LEONARD BERNSTEIN

The Man,

His Work,

and

His World

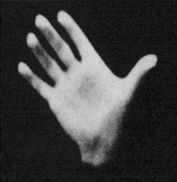

LEONARD

CLEVELAND AND NEW YORK

The Man,

His Work,

and

His World

BERNSTEIN

by

John Briggs

THE WORLD PUBLISHING COMPANY

PUBLISHED BY The World Publishing Company
2231 WEST 110TH STREET, CLEVELAND 2, OHIO

PUBLISHED SIMULTANEOUSLY IN CANADA BY
NELSON, FOSTER & SCOTT LTD.

Library of Congress Catalog Card Number: 61-10167

FIRST EDITION

"Class Song" music by Leonard Bernstein and words by
Leonard Bernstein and Lawrence F. Ebb is reproduced
by permission of Amberson Enterprises, Inc.,
copyright owner. Copyright © 1961 by Amberson
Enterprises, Inc. G. Schirmer, Inc. sole licensing agent.

TO

J. G. B.

Introduction

FOR HIS ASTONISHING VERSATILITY as performer, composer, teacher, essayist, and TV music lecturer to the nation, and for the wide-ranging scope of his restless intelligence, Leonard Bernstein has often been compared to a Renaissance Man.

That is apt but not exact. Bernstein is the Renaissance Man from Boston. At home on five continents and in five languages, the cosmopolitan has not lost the Yankee practicality which is a part of his New England heritage. An earlier Renaissance Man might expend valuable time in designing submarines which would not submerge, aircraft which would not fly, and in his own lifetime see his "Last Supper" begin to disintegrate as a consequence of his obstinate experiments in mixing pigments; the modern Renaissance Man has a genuine flair for getting things done and his whole career is proof of how nothing succeeds like success. He does not, like Palestrina, turn aside from the writing of heavenly motets to make a fortune in the fur business; the nearest he has gotten to Seventh Avenue is the stage door of the Metropolitan Opera House.

"Genius," said yet another Renaissance Man, "is perfection in trifles; but perfection is no trifle." If "genius" seems a premature word for Bernstein at this stage of his career, the quotation is one which springs to mind when, for example, watching him go through a score at rehearsal to correct errors in the orchestra parts. It is dull, tedious, and exasperating work; but it has to be done, and Bernstein brings to it the same energy and concentration which he lavishes on a television performance. Both TV lecture and musical proofreading, moreover, are manifestations of the New England schoolmaster's temperament which is an important part of his artistic personality.

If Bernstein has not, with the somewhat repetitious versatility of the Renaissance Man, turned aside from his chosen art to experiment with drainage canals and military fortifications, within the framework of his art he is a bundle of paradoxes. A showman who can speak the language and write the music of Broadway, he is also an earnest, thoroughly trained musician. Having, in his own words, the performer's compulsion to "get out there and let it out" in front of the public, he is of an essentially scholarly temperament, valuing the hours spent in his study and wishing he could find time for more. In a calling whose performers, to paraphrase Sheridan, often "play like an angel and talk like Poor Poll," Bernstein is adept at writing and speaking lucid prose. And its lucidity is based on knowledge. He writes of jazz not as a square condescending to take a turn at an unfamiliar medium, but as a working jazzman since high school days. His comments on Bach are the fruit of longtime study, not only of the music but also of the composer's life and times. His essay on Bach the numerologist surprised and fascinated many who thought they already knew their *St. Matthew Passion* pretty well. He writes on conducting as a conductor, performance as a performer, composition as a composer. Except for the fact that nature has given him a conductor's voice, Bernstein is not far from being The Compleat Musician.

Most paradoxical of all is that musical lightning should strike in a non-musical, suburban American household. Prodigious feats of musicality are more usually performed by those who are second to tenth generation musicians and receive their first instructions from father or mother at the age of three.

The portrait of a living figure can never be quite exact, especially when, as in Bernstein's case,

11

he is in mid-career with every sign of having still a long way to go. Only the death-mask is final. An attempt has been made here to assess Bernstein from many points of view, recording the impressions of those who know him now and those who knew him when, those who value the pleasure of his company and those who have had the more strenuous relationship of working collaboration, those who like him and those who don't.

Always there has been an attempt to weigh bias, pro or con. The most amusing version of the story is not necessarily the most accurate one.

The manager of a Midwestern orchestra once told how the orchestra's irascible conductor suddenly decided life was not worth living without a black limousine with white-sidewall tires. This would have presented no particular problem except that postwar production had just been resumed, every ounce of steel and every pair of experienced hands was wanted on the assembly line to satisfy pent-up demand, and nobody wanted to take time out for the time-consuming luxury of handcrafting a limousine.

Nevertheless, a conscientious orchestral board of directors will do anything within reason to keep the maestro happy. Somebody made a swap of ball bearings for steel, one thing led to another and in freezing sub-zero weather the orchestra manager went to Detroit to bring back the car. With the satisfaction of a difficult mission accomplished, he parked it outside the conductor's apartment.

The conductor came down to look, and dismissed it with a wave of his hand. "Too big, don't want it, take it away."

If this story were told on Bernstein, it would not be funny because nobody would believe it. Although, like any public figure, he has been the target for gossip and scuttlebutt, in one area there is a void. Detractors and defenders all agree on this point—Bernstein is not a prima donna. Perhaps he has not had time to be.

Although the pages which follow are in no sense an authorized biography, its long-suffering central figure has taken time out from his hectic winter season to sit for his portrait, so to speak, clarifying and elucidating matters which were obscure or doubtful. Helen Coates, almost as reliable an authority on the conductor as Bernstein himself, was enormously helpful. Jack Gottlieb, Bernstein's assistant and his former pupil at Brandeis University, had interesting recollections of Bernstein as university professor.

Special thanks are due to Bernstein's family; to Samuel Bernstein, for making available to World's editors an interesting selection of boyhood pictures, and to Shirley Bernstein, for recollections of the early days and for setting straight several matters which had been garbled in previous publication.

Carlos Moseley of the New York Philharmonic, Jerome Toobin of the Symphony of the Air, Alan Kayes of RCA Victor, and Jack Frizzell of Columbia Records were helpful sources of information on Bernstein as seen from the vantage-point of orchestra and recording management. In this group, too, should be included Steve Rosenfeld, a former member of the Philharmonic staff whose sharp reporter's eye brought back vivid impressions of the tour of the USSR.

For recollections of Bernstein's student days I am indebted to Dr. André C. Vauclain, Jane Fairfax Hill and my wife, all of the Curtis Institute faculty, and to various fellow students both in Boston and Philadelphia.

Bernstein's name has been in the air since November 14, 1943. Even before that he was known and believed in by Henry W. Simon, now Bernstein's publisher and then a fellow critic, whose estimate of Bernstein's talents time has shown to be remarkably correct. At various times I have sympathized with his editorial perplexity as to when Bernstein would get around to finishing a book of essays called *Conversations at Thirty*. The Conversations, ten years late but none the worse for that, turned up in Bernstein's book, *The Joy of Music*.

Constance Hope, who on behalf of RCA Victor signed Bernstein to his first recording contract, and has remained a close friend of the Bernsteins, as long-time confidante afforded a particularly interesting point of view toward the artist. For Bernstein as seen by his publishers I am indebted among others to H. W. Heinsheimer of G. Schirmer, Inc. Martin Feinstein of the S. Hurok organization, Margaret Carson and Friede F. Rothe have been helpful not only for their own impressions but also those of artists who have performed with Bernstein. Arthur V. Berger, who went from the New York *Herald Tribune* to Brandeis University, and who was on cordial terms with the late Serge Koussevitzky, has supplied interesting footnotes to the Koussevitzkyan phase of Bernstein's career. And for a point of view on Bernstein as seen by a superbly professional colleague special thanks are due to Hershy Kay, who, since the days of *On the Town,* has worked closely with Bernstein on a number of musicals.

The list could be continued. Former student Samuel Krachmalnick and fellow composer Morton Gould, longtime friend and collaborator Jennie Tourel, violinist Isaac Stern and pianist Leonid Hambro are some of the co-workers who in various ways have helped to round out the portrait of Bernstein as man and artist. For revealing insights into Bernstein's impact as a TV personality, the Robert Saudek organization has been of great assistance.

Finally, thanks are due to William Targ of The World Publishing Company, who lightened the drudgery of authorship by unfailing sympathy and moral support; and to his assistant, Lee Griffin, whose pursuit of picture credits began at the New York *Times* photo morgue (aided by Tess Kaufman McCafferey of the *Times* music department) and continued, quite literally, around the world.

LEONARD BERNSTEIN

The Man,

His Work,

and

His World

Chapter 1

IN MID-SEPTEMBER, 1939, when World War II was hardly a month old, a twenty-one-year-old Bostonian, Harvard '39, A. B. *cum laude in musica*, with the unmistakable look of the hay-fever sufferer on his lean, expressive face, walked into the mellow old-Philadelphia Common Room of the Curtis Institute of Music. He was immediately ushered into the formidable presence of Fritz Reiner, head of the Institute's orchestral department.

The appointment with Reiner was out of season. Normally, one would audition for Reiner's conducting class in April rather than September. But exceptions could always be made, especially when Dimitri Mitropoulos, conductor of the Minneapolis Symphony Orchestra, asked his good friend Reiner to hear a wonderfully promising Harvard boy, Leonard Bernstein by name.

Reiner wasted little time on amenities. On the piano music rack, spread open so that its title page was not visible, was an orchestral score.

"Play this," Reiner commanded, "and tell me what it is."

Bernstein flexed his fingers, rusty from a summer of little practicing, studied the page for a moment, and set to work.

Here a word demands to be said about reading at sight from a full orchestral score. It is a feat which not every musician, even a good one, can manage. So great an artist as the late Josef Hofmann was a notoriously poor sight reader who even found it difficult to cope with the two staves on which piano music is written. Instead of two, an orchestral score may be on fifteen staves or more. In addition to the familiar treble and bass, it employs alto and tenor clefs. A further brain-scrambling complication is added by the transposing instruments, whose music sounds in a different key from that in which it is written.

Reading a full score is roughly equivalent to reading fifteen lines of type in several different languages printed one above the other, and keeping them all straight in one's mind. Like playing chess blindfold or juggling nine billiard balls, it is not beyond human attainment; but it requires a certain flair and constant practice.

Grappling with the score set before him, Bernstein noticed a bouncy little tune in the wood-winds, a traditional "freshman song" of the German universities. In a Boston public school, Bernstein had sung it to the words:

> What clatters on the roof
> With quick impatient hoof?
> I think it must be Santa Claus,
> Dear old Santa Claus . . .

"Brahms!" Bernstein exclaimed. *"The Academic Festival Overture."*

"Very good," said Reiner. "Now play it to the end."

When the music ended with a brilliant flourish of "Gaudeamus Igitur," Reiner questioned the gifted young sight reader about his past musical experience and plans for the future. The answers were satisfactory, and Bernstein was in.

A few days later, there were other examinations and auditions, as a result of which Bernstein could send word home to Boston that he had been accepted as a conducting student by Reiner, as a piano student by Isabelle Vengerova, and as an orchestration student by composer Randall Thompson, who had just succeeded Josef Hofmann as head of the school.

The Harvard boy had made good, and began apartment-hunting in the neighborhood of Rittenhouse Square.

Considering how far and how fast it has taken him, Bernstein's talent was rather late in manifesting itself. Musicians often begin as child prodigies. An illustrative story is of a turn-of-the-century meeting between violinist Bronislaw Hubermann and pianist Artur Rubinstein. "You have talent, my child," Hubermann told the younger player. "Work hard and you will go far." Hubermann was then nine, Rubinstein four.

At ten, one is, by ordinary rules of thumb, too old to think of a virtuoso career. However, this was the age at which Bernstein had his first direct contact with music.

The oldest of three children, Bernstein was born in Lawrence, Massachusetts, on August 25, 1918. Both his parents were Russian immigrants. Samuel Bernstein's first job in this country had been scaling fish in the shadow of the Brooklyn Bridge for one dollar a day. Soon he succeeded in "getting into hair," working in an establishment which manufactured "rats" and "waterfalls." By the time Leonard arrived on the scene, his father had transferred his activities to Boston and was building up a prosperous beauty parlor and barber supply business. When Leonard was less than a year old, the family moved from Lawrence, a rather grim New England mill town, to a comfortable residential neighborhood in Boston.

Bernstein was ten when the great turning point

in his life occurred. His Aunt Clara had been divorced and was moving to a small apartment. Her large upright piano could not be accommodated there. Would the Bernsteins care to keep it?

Coming home from school one day, Bernstein saw the piano and sat down to try it out. It was, he recalls, "love at first sight." He began playing, and liked what he heard. The upshot was that every moment which could be spared from schoolwork he spent exploring the fascinating world of sound which the piano made available to his curious fingers. Soon the piano was more than just a new interest; it was an obsession. He played until all hours. His sister Shirley, who was then five, remembers going to sleep every night to the sound of her brother's music in the living room.

His parents were somewhat perplexed by their eldest son's new-found talent. Neither had much interest in music; Samuel Bernstein had obtained his first impression of it from tatterdemalion Klezmir fiddlers in his native village in the Russian province of Rovno. Judged by that standard, music was a calling which conferred neither wealth nor distinction upon its practitioners.

But since it was obvious that at the moment music meant more to his son than anything else, Samuel Bernstein agreed to let the boy take lessons.

Of his first piano teacher, Friede Karp, Bernstein remembers that she was beautiful and that her fee was only one dollar per lesson. After two years' study, to his disappointment, she married and moved to California.

Bernstein's next teacher came near to finishing him as a pianist. One of those musicians obsessed by a "method," she believed that the pianist's fingers should be held flat above the keys, not arched at the knuckles. She was undeterred by the fact that it would have been difficult, then as now, to cite an outstanding or even passable performer who played piano in accordance with the "method."

For almost two years, Bernstein tried to play in this cramped, artificial manner. He believes now that, if he had continued much longer, his technique would have been irretrievably ruined.

Even then, it was clear to the fourteen-year-old pianist that he was going up a blind alley. Disengaging himself from the "method," he sought the advice of Heinrich Gebhard, Boston's foremost piano teacher.

Gebhard recommended Helen Coates, an auburn-haired, blue-eyed lady from Rockford, Illinois, who had come East to study with Gebhard and stayed on as his assistant.

Helen Coates's most striking trait is an imperturbability not shaken by any amount of stress and strain. This quality has proved valuable in the later, more hectic phase of her association with Bernstein.

Even in the beginning, Miss Coates found her new pupil extraordinary and sometimes exasperating. He spent every spare moment playing, listening to music, or composing it. His appetite for music was insatiable. In addition to assigned pieces, he had explored the repertory of piano and other music on his own, and had gone through an impressive number of the works available at the Newton, Massachusetts, Public Library.

Although he had had no systematic instruction in music theory, as a result of his wide-ranging curiosity, Bernstein had discovered for himself the tonal system which is the cornerstone of Western music. That after four years' study one should be innocent of this basic musical concept does not reflect much credit on the quality of Bernstein's early training. His innate musicality, however, was shown by the fact that he perceived the tonic-dominant relationship and felt it important enough to deserve a name. Not knowing the usual terminology, he invented his own. The keynote or tonic, the point of stability at which a piece usually begins and ends, he called the "finishing chord." (Years later, in a TV lecture, he would compare it to "home base.") The dominant fifth, which in every key exerts a pull toward the tonic almost like the force of gravity, he called the "governing chord."

There was another chord, too, he noted, which pulled toward the tonic, although not quite so forcefully, in the form of a plagal or "Amen" cadence. His name for this was the "vice-governing chord."

Miss Coates listened with interest to Bernstein's account of his musical discoveries, and kept a straight face when he brought to his lesson an enormous Piano Concerto compounded of equal parts of Liszt and Tchaikovsky. (Later, Bernstein referred to this youthful effusion as "the Russo-Gypsy War.")

Miss Coates did not schedule anyone else after Bernstein's lesson. The nominally hour-long sessions often extended to three hours or more. From the beginning, a strong bond of sympathy existed between teacher and pupil. Fascinated by Bernstein's lively and wide-ranging intelligence, Miss Coates gave motherly advice on musical and non-musical matters, including the poetry which Bernstein was beginning to write.

Affection for her gifted pupil did not blind Miss Coates to flaws in his musical equipment. He was a fluent but erratic player. He hated the drudgery of scales, arpeggios, and five-finger exercises. Nevertheless, Miss Coates saw to it that he drudged. A voracious sight reader, he could get the general idea at a glance and was impatient with the tedious filing and polishing of musical detail which full mastery of a piano work requires. Miss Coates took care of that, too.

A curious fact was that Bernstein's preoccupation with music did not interfere with his studies along other lines. In fact it seemed to be the other way around. He recalls that until he was ten, he was "a scared, skinny, sickly kid," plagued with asthma and loser of decision after decision to other boys in the neighborhood. But through music, he seemed suddenly and dramatically to have found his bearings. Whether or not it was cause and effect, the trend thereafter was upward.

At Boston Latin School, the pride of the city's public school system, Bernstein made good grades and, having organized his own jazz band, was a social lion as well.

His family observed his progress with both pride and misgivings. Like anyone who has started a business from scratch and seen it prosper, Samuel Bernstein had tucked in the back of his mind the pleasant thought that one day his son would take over the company. But the current of young Bernstein's life was sweeping farther and farther from beauty parlor supplies.

Today, Samuel Bernstein dislikes being reminded that he opposed, even briefly, his son's musical career.

"It pains him," says Shirley Bernstein, who has vivid memories of family squabbles on this point. "He has shut it out. He doesn't like to remember it. But he did; *he did.*"

At one point, the elder Bernstein halted the piano lessons by cutting off his son's allowance. The halt was only temporary, however. Soon, word got round that Sam Bernstein's boy was playing in a dance band at two dollars a night to earn money for music lessons. That put matters on a different footing, one of family and neighborhood pride, and the allowance was restored.

Actually, in ninety-nine cases out of a hundred, Samuel Bernstein's advice would have been the best a father could have given and his son would have done well to heed it. The overcrowded musical field is precarious unless one's natural gifts, like Bernstein's, are so vehemently specialized for music as to make any other calling unthinkable.

Six summer weeks in the stockroom confirmed beyond all doubt that Bernstein and his father's business were not meant for each other.

But to Samuel Bernstein's credit, it must be noted that he bowed gracefully to the inevitable. On a special occasion, he even took his son to hear Sergei Rachmaninoff play a recital at Symphony Hall. It was the first live concert either of them had attended.

Samuel Bernstein, moreover, could not have failed to be impressed when his son was piano soloist with the Boston Public School Orchestra; or when, during a Caribbean cruise, he was offered a job as shipboard pianist.

An even more Protean display of talent, fore-shadowing the later Bernstein, took place at Sharon, Massachusetts, where the Bernsteins had a summer home. Among other things, Bernstein produced, directed, helped write English lyrics for, and, in a wig and black shawl, played the title role in *Carmen*.

Bernstein's string of successes is broken in only one place: although he has entered many contests, he has never won a first prize. One often-told story is of his entering a contest for young conductors and missing the first prize of five hundred dollars but winning the second, an all-expenses-paid week-end at Tanglewood. Bernstein was then a student conductor at Tanglewood.

Se non è vero, è ben trovato . . . Bernstein did enter such a contest while at Tanglewood, earning the right to conduct the Boston Pops Orchestra in the Prelude to *Die Meistersinger*. Otherwise, he has been singularly unfortunate as a contestant.

What Bernstein considers to have been a major turning point in his life occurred one Saturday evening when he was sixteen. He tuned in the Boston Symphony Orchestra broadcast and for the first time heard Prokofiev's "Classical" Symphony and Stravinsky's *Sacre du printemps*. The gay in-souciance of the Prokofiev work, with its clever tongue-in-cheek parody of the Mozart-Haydn style, made him burst out laughing. As for the Stravin-

"Class Song" music by Leonard Bernstein and words by Leonard Bernstein and Lawrence F. Ebb is reproduced by permission of Amberson Enterprises, Inc., copyright owner. Copyright © 1961 by Amberson Enterprises, Inc. G. Schirmer, Inc. sole licensing agent.

sky, its pulsating energy and fierce driving rhythms were like nothing Bernstein had ever heard before. "Up till then," he recalls, "I had never realized music had a future."

This turned his interest toward the theories of atonality and polytonality, on the basis of which Stravinsky and his contemporaries had taken their bold departure from the musical styles of the nineteenth century. Bernstein even composed a piano sonatina of his own in the newly discovered "modern idiom."

In 1935, Bernstein graduated "with distinction" from the Boston Latin School. The Class of '35 was the three hundredth to leave the school, and this milestone was marked with appropriate ceremony. Not the least impressive feature was the class song, with music by Leonard Bernstein and words by Leonard Bernstein and Lawrence F. Ebb. It is here published for the first time.

Chapter 2

$\mathcal{A}$LTHOUGH BERNSTEIN entered Harvard as a music major, he took as few music courses as he could get by with, and as many courses in philosophy and languages as he could find time for. This arrangement worked so well that he graduated *cum laude* four years later.

At Harvard, Bernstein had his first systematic training in harmony, learning that musicians had long known about the "vice-governing chord" and the "finishing chord." He also studied counterpoint and orchestration, and had the stimulating experience of association with the composers Walter Piston and Edward Burlingame Hill.

By now, Bernstein had graduated from Miss Coates to Heinrich Gebhard himself. Gebhard, no partisan of the contemporary musical idiom, was visibly taken aback when Bernstein brought in Aaron Copland's ferociously difficult and dissonant Piano Variations.

It was under Gebhard's supervision that Bernstein learned the Ravel Piano Concerto in G, a work in which he has often appeared as conductor-soloist and which he maintains he could play if suddenly awakened from a sound sleep.

His studies left Bernstein sufficient time and energy to accompany the college glee club; to write, direct, and perform in various Class Day skits; and to compose and conduct an hour of music for a Harvard Classical Club performance, in the original Greek, of Aristophanes's *The Birds*.

The Aristophanes music is an early Bernstein score of more than passing interest; a good deal of it later turned up in Bernstein's first hit musical, *On the Town*.

Bernstein's most ambitious Harvard project was to stage the first Boston performance of Marc Blitzstein's play with music, *The Cradle Will Rock*. Bernstein had seen the New York production and, back at Harvard, began rounding up the necessary talent. He cast his sister Shirley in the role of a prostitute, to their mutual amusement and their family's dismay.

Originally, Bernstein's plan had been to present *The Cradle Will Rock* in a Boston theater. City authorities objected on the grounds that the work was "obscene." But the censor's authority did not extend to Harvard. The performance took place at Sanders Theater. Seated at a piano on stage, exactly as composer Blitzstein had done in the New York production, Bernstein played and conducted the singers. ("He did it better than I did," said Blitzstein, who had come up for the Harvard performance.) The Boston critics turned out, and conductor-pianist-co-director Bernstein had to his credit another personal triumph.

Bernstein himself occasionally had a fling at criticism, writing in Harvard's literary publication, the *Advocate*. Of a concert by Serge Koussevitzky and the Boston Symphony Orchestra, he wrote:

By and large it was the traditional BSO offering: magnificent precision, the unbreakable tradition of wrong notes in the French horn department, the phenomenon (in the Vivaldi) of seeing woodwinds blown and not hearing them, the remarkable industry of the percussion boys, Our Director's most individualistic conception of tempi—all the things we have come to know and love. One innovation, however; Dr. Koussevitzky has added a tenth bull fiddle, so that the Scherzo of Beethoven's Fifth had something of Fate in it after all.

In view of the close and cordial relations later to exist between Koussevitzky and Bernstein, it must be concluded that Koussevitzky either did

34

not read the review or was amused by its brashness. At any rate, he harbored no ill will toward its outspoken author.

During Harvard vacations, Bernstein worked at a variety of odd jobs, one of them as music counselor at Camp Onota, near Pittsfield, Massachusetts. For a performance of *The Pirates of Penzance* under Bernstein's direction, a Bronx youngster named Adolph Green had been invited up to do the Pirate King. Mutual friends told Bernstein that Green possessed a knowledge of music which was truly phenomenal. He could sing nearly any work in the concert repertoire straight through.

Bernstein thereupon prepared for Green one of those elaborate practical jokes dear to the hearts of musicians. As soon as possible after they met, he lured Green to a piano and brought up the matter of a certain "Shostakovitch prelude."

"Which one?" Green inquired.

"This one," Bernstein replied. Sitting down at the piano, he played a jarring series of dissonances.

Running through the works of Shostakovitch in his mind, Green furrowed his brow and said he could not place any such Shostakovitch prelude.

Bernstein practically fell on his neck with delight. This man was no phony. Everyone else for whom he had played the spurious work had "recognized" it.

The friendship with Green which began at

Camp Onota was to have important consequences for Bernstein's career later on. So was another chance meeting of his Harvard days, with the conductor Dimitri Mitropoulos.

There have been points in Bernstein's career at which it has been difficult for him to resist the conclusion that the hand of destiny is on his shoulder. One such occasion was in January, 1937, when Mitropoulos was making an appearance as guest conductor of the Boston Symphony Orchestra.

For Bernstein to have met Mitropoulos would have been relatively simple. He need only have gone to the green room, for example, where a conductor traditionally receives homage after a concert. Bernstein did not do so. If anything, he went out of his way not to seek a meeting with Mitropoulos. Yet it happened, through the workings of a long series of coincidences, as if foreordained.

How the meeting came about is reconstructed by Bernstein as follows. On Saturday afternoon, in the common room of Eliot House, he met an acquaintance who invited him to a party in Brookline that evening.

Bernstein had already made a date to take a girl to the Boston Symphony concert. He said politely that they would drop in at the party if they could, although he had not the slightest intention of doing so.

On the way home from the concert, however, his father's car ran out of gas in Brookline. He had it filled at a service station which turned out to be just around the corner from where the party was taking place. They decided to look in on it.

The party proved to be a dull affair and they did not stay long. As they were leaving, another acquaintance, just arriving, mentioned that the Harvard Hellenic Society was holding a reception for Mitropoulos the next afternoon at Phillips Brooks House. Bernstein noted the fact absent-mindedly; he planned to spend Sunday with his family.

Next day, after hearing the Philharmonic broadcast, Bernstein, oppressed by the proximity of mid-year exams, decided to go back to school early to study. His mother, after urging him to stay, put on a fur coat over her house dress to drive him to Harvard.

The jokes about Boston's winding streets have a solid basis in fact. Even Bostonians can get lost there, and as a result of a wrong turn, Mrs. Bernstein found herself in front of Phillips Brooks House. Being there, Bernstein decided that they might as well look in on the reception.

They found themselves in a hot, overcrowded room listening to a Concertino for Flute and

Piano by Chaminade. Mrs. Bernstein did not dare take off her fur coat, and they were both so oppressed by the heat, the crowd, and Chaminade that they were on the point of leaving.

Then, as the last in the long chain of coincidences, the Concertino ended, a receiving line formed and Bernstein found himself experiencing at first hand what he later called "the incredible hypnotic quality of this man."

Mitropoulos for his part was impressed by Bernstein, especially when fellow undergraduates passed the word that Bernstein was a better than passable pianist. After the receiving-line amenities were finished, Bernstein was prevailed upon to play—a Chopin nocturne and the final movement of his own Sonatina.

A long and absorbing conversation with Mitropoulos followed, during which the conductor was somewhat staggered to learn the scope and diversity of Bernstein's musical activities The sequel was that he invited Bernstein to attend that week's rehearsals of the Boston Symphony Orchestra.

Bernstein spent the week walking on air and letting midyears take care of themselves. The orchestra rehearsals were a revelation. For the first time, he began to have a sense of the intricate, delicately poised relationship between a conductor and a major symphony orchestra.

"Not that I had the faintest idea of conducting

myself," he says. "It all seemed too glamorous and remote."

Nevertheless, it was less remote, now that he was behind the scenes, watching a performance being put together. And in Mitropoulos he had a fascinating object lesson in conductorial psychology. Mitropoulos represented a complete break with the tradition of the "shouting conductor." For all his frenetic weaving and flailing of the air at a performance, Mitropoulos in rehearsal had none of the incandescent fury of Toscanini, or the red-faced rage of Koussevitzky. He cajoled; he exhorted; he took the musicians into his confidence.

Endowed with a phenomenal memory, which he had further developed by incessant practice, Mitropoulos conducted without a score. He corrected every slip, every wrong note by the orchestra, from memory.

As if scores were not enough, Mitropoulos also memorized personnel lists. This really impressed the players. Most conductors know by name the concertmaster and some of the key players; but when a visiting conductor addresses a fourth-chair violinist or a second bassoon by name, as Mitropoulos did, the effect on the orchestra must be seen to be believed.

Sitting in darkened Symphony Hall, Bernstein watched with avidity all that went on, unconsciously making notes for future guidance. His great moment came when Mitropoulos took him to lunch, called him "genius boy," and introduced him to oysters.

Upon his graduation from Harvard in June, 1939, Bernstein faced the same dilemma as did most of his classmates. He had a diploma but no job. It was to be through Mitropoulos that he found a solution.

Samuel Bernstein had indicated that a job was still waiting in the family business. He had also made it clear that he was not greatly interested in subsidizing a musical career for his gifted but unbusinesslike son.

Father and son finally reached a compromise. Since there appeared to be no demand for his talents in Boston, Bernstein would try his luck in New York. He could stay there until the end of the summer. After that . . .

Bernstein accepted eagerly, although the plan was heavily in his disfavor. Of all times of the year for doing business in New York music circles, there is none less propitious than summer. Nearly everybody is out of town; those who are not say: "See me after Labor Day."

Nevertheless, Bernstein hopefully descended upon Manhattan and lost no time looking up his friend of Camp Onota days, Adolph Green. He and Green took an apartment together in Greenwich Village.

Green at this time was a member of the Revuers, a satiric group which performed in a cellar night-club called the Village Vanguard. Others of the five members were Betty Comden and Judy Holliday. All were bright, eager, hopeful, and unknown. The group's appeal was not so much in its vocalism as in its "special material," smart, satirical verses lampooning foibles of the day. All five members took a hand in writing them, with Comden and Green showing a special affinity for the work.

From the first, the Revuers had a small, fanatically loyal following. Eventually they caught on, moving from the Village Vanguard to the Rainbow Room in Radio City. But that was much later, after Bernstein and the Revuers had, for the time being, gone their separate ways.

During his first summer in New York, however, Bernstein spent many evenings at the Vanguard, often filling in as pianist for the Revuers. Performing with this lively troupe helped to divert his thoughts from his lack of success in the more serious concert world.

By September, Bernstein had been in New York three months, and New York could not have cared less. His alternatives appeared to be to sell beauty parlor equipment, or to starve. Bernstein had no intention of starving; he had already been near enough to doing so. Finally, when he was down to his last four dollars, he bought a clarinet in a pawnshop and dejectedly made plans to return to Boston.

There, fate once more stepped in, via a chance meeting with a Harvard classmate who happened to mention that Mitropoulos was just back from Europe and was staying at the Hotel Biltmore.

Bernstein at once drove back to New York to call on Mitropoulos, who was delighted to see the "genius boy" again.

"I had a long talk with Dimitri," Bernstein recalls. "I told him I was hung up. I was finished with school and didn't know what to do next.

"He said, 'You ought to be a conductor.'

"I said, 'What makes you say that?'

"He said, 'I just sense it—you have everything a conductor should have.'

"I said, 'How do you become a conductor?'

"He said, 'You have to go to a school, like Juilliard.' "

Bernstein applied to Juilliard next day and got a discouraging answer. It was September and no more applications were being accepted. On Mitropoulos's advice, he next approached the Curtis Institute.

Here he found arrangements to be more flexible. Reiner would test candidates for his conducting class whenever a promising aspirant turned up. That Bernstein came with a recommendation from Mitropoulos also helped.

In retrospect, the chance encounter with Mitropoulos appears to have been a moment of crucial importance to Bernstein's career. At the time, however, he was chiefly concerned with how to persuade Samuel Bernstein that there were things to be gained from the Curtis Institute above and beyond what Harvard had to offer.

Chapter 3

BERNSTEIN is remembered by some of his Curtis Institute fellow students as moody and preoccupied; by others as a gifted, wildly undisciplined youngster who had not yet learned to harness his considerable talents.

Both by his own testimony and that of his classmates, Bernstein did not greatly enjoy his years at the Curtis Institute. Not everyone does, especially those who come to it from the wholly different world of a college or university campus. At best, there is in retrospect a certain grim satisfaction, like that of the desert nomad, at having triumphed over an environment in which not everyone would be able to survive.

As a college graduate, Bernstein found himself in a decided minority group. "I was treated as a freak," he says. Far more typical were the child prodigies who had entered the school at the age of ten or twelve. As a training school modeled rather closely on the lines of the Paris Conservatory, the Institute was severely functional. Philosophical discussions of the sort which Bernstein had relished at Harvard were rare. What had Plato's *Symposium* to do with playing the Glazunov Concerto?

During his directorate, Randall Thompson made an attempt to transform the Institute into less of a conservatory and more of a university. But one cannot have it both ways. A university is difficult to form with students of such diverse ages and cultural backgrounds. The Institute was, and remains, a superbly professional school where gifted performers undergo the hard disciplines that make an artist.

From Bernstein's point of view, a further shortcoming of the Curtis Institute was that it was in Philadelphia. Boston meant home and family; New York was exciting; but Philadelphia, however full of mellow charm for the antiquarian, was rather poky after Greenwich Village.

But Bernstein's working schedule, in a school to which one was admitted only through competitive examinations, and in which one was assumed to be a genius until proved otherwise, left little time for self-pity.

45

First and foremost were the lessons with Reiner, a stern taskmaster whose idea of a light weekend assignment was mastering, say, the "Leonore" Overture No. 3 so faultlessly that at whatever point requested the student could name the note being played by every instrument.

Reiner's perpetual scowl and his biting sarcasm were famous. By a single withering comment he had been known to reduce an entire orchestra to helpless, quivering fury.

Nor were composers exempt. Once when a new opera was being prepared, the composer stopped the orchestra repeatedly to explain how the music should go. By the end of the long rehearsal, Reiner's patience was wearing thin.

When the composer took what Reiner considered an unreasonable amount of time over a passage for the French horns, Reiner cut the explanation short.

"In other words," he told the orchestra, "play it the way you always play it in *Rosenkavalier*."

So famous was the whiplash of Reiner's tongue that Reiner himself had a wry joke about it.

"Not all the players in the orchestra hated me," he would say of this or that city. "Only the bad musicians."

Reiner's conception of conducting differed markedly from that of, say, Toscanini, who had never had a lesson and made it clear that he did not propose to train apprentices. Other conductors, too,

46

a rather surprising number of whom have had no formal training in this branch of music, have held conducting to be an intuitive thing which one can either do fairly easily or not at all, and have doubted that it could be learned through formal study.

Reiner's position was that it could be learned, and would be learned, if he had to knock it into his students with a sledge hammer.

The goal toward which Reiner propelled his students was mastery of stick technique. Through years of experimentation, he had perfected a set of semaphore signals which was the marvel of orchestral players everywhere for the clarity with which it conveyed what the conductor wanted. It was Reiner's boast that, having mastered his system, a student could stand up before an orchestra anywhere in the Western world and, without speaking a single word, make his intentions clear by hand and baton signals alone.

The interaction of Reiner and Bernstein upon each other was fruitful. Reiner remembers Bernstein as his all-around most gifted pupil. Bernstein for his part speaks of his former teacher with devotion and admiration.

Bernstein, it is true, could not be brought forward as a model disciple of the Reiner system. Reiner's tight, economical beat did not suit his ardent temperament. As for stick technique, until

47

he became musical director of the Philharmonic, he did not even use a baton, conducting with his hands in the Stokowski manner.

Nevertheless, the years of study with Reiner left their mark on Bernstein both as conductor and musician, even if not directly reflected in his conducting style. They might be compared with a foundation wall laid on a bedrock which is none the less important for not being visible on the surface.

Hardly less formidable than Reiner was Mme. Vengerova, of whom Bernstein was in terror during his first few student months.

Study with Vengerova was a very practical application of what Josef Hofmann stated as the purpose of the Curtis Institute: "To hand down through contemporary masters the great traditions of the past."

Vengerova was a solid link with the Great Traditions. She had studied with Theodore Leschetizky, teacher of Paderewski, Gabrilowitsch, Mark Hambourg, Artur Schnabel, Ethel Leginska, Fannie Bloomfield-Zeisler, and other outstanding performers, including Bernstein's Harvard teacher, Heinrich Gebhard. And for good measure, Vengerova had studied with Annette Essipova, the lady virtuoso who had electrified London audiences in the nineties (G. B. Shaw, then music critic of the *Star*, compared her rapid passages with "a dextrous whip-cut along the keyboard") and who also had been the second of Leschetizky's four wives.

Vengerova students shared a common virtue: technique. While one might question their interpretation of this or that particular passage, no one could deny that they possessed good fingers. They achieved this in a very simple way. They worked. Hard.

Vengerova bore down especially hard on the new boy from Harvard. Long afterward, Bernstein found out why.

He had auditioned for Rudolf Serkin, who was then away on a concert tour. Applicants for Serkin's classes were being heard by a board of judges of which Vengerova was a member.

Rusty from lack of practice, Bernstein "hacked my way," as he puts it, through a Bach prelude and fugue. In the backstage discussion which followed, the board was divided, Vengerova alone maintaining that Bernstein had potential. Finally, Vengerova resolved the impasse by announcing that she would add Bernstein to her own schedule.

After that, Bernstein had to produce.

Compared with Gebhard, study with Vengerova was like a cold plunge. Gebhard, a courtly European, had couched every criticism in such terms as: "My dear boy, it's beautiful, but don't you think . . ." Vengerova was more direct: "How *dare* you make an accent there—just because your thumb is on the note!"

Despite her severity, Bernstein ended by being as enchanted as everyone else with Vengerova. He feels that the greatest single contribution she made to his musical development was in forcing him to listen to his own playing. Simple and obvious as this seems, it is easier said than done. Mechanical repetition of a phrase can lead to mechanical playing. Bernstein's conviction, to which a regular concertgoer can only say Amen, is that not listening to themselves is the most frequent reason for the unmusicality of unmusical pianists.

Bernstein approached counterpoint from a different, more traditional point of view. At Harvard, his teacher, A. Tillman Merritt, had used a system of his own. Bernstein had never heard of the five species of counterpoint until he entered the Institute.

He became a pupil in orchestration of Randall Thompson when the composer assured him he had a great gift for instrumental writing.

"But I've never written anything," Bernstein objected.

Thompson said that did not matter; his flair was obvious.

The lessons in orchestration were the beginning of a warm and enduring friendship. Thompson and Bernstein shared fondness for the abstruse puzzles found in British newspapers. At lessons, Thompson would begin the two-hour session by sneaking out of his desk the latest issue of the London *Times*. Only when they had worked the puzzle would they turn to orchestration.

At Curtis, Bernstein excelled in many areas, becoming the bright particular star of the score-reading class conducted by Renée Longy Miquelle. But the major influences were those of Reiner and Vengerova. In retrospect, Bernstein doubts whether he could have found anywhere two teachers more valuable to him at that particular stage of his career.

A third name was added at the end of his first year at Curtis. As part of the Berkshire Music Festival for 1940, Serge Koussevitzky had planned to invite three or four promising youngsters to spend the summer with him studying conducting. Bernstein's application, backed by letters of recommendation from Reiner and Mitropoulos, was one of those accepted.

When Bernstein wrote his somewhat ironic opinion of "Our Director" for the Harvard *Advocate,* he had never met Koussevitzky in person. He found the meeting a heady experience. Koussevitzky radiated charm in all directions. His personality magnetized orchestra directors and women's groups to such an extent that insofar as the Boston Symphony Orchestra was concerned, his word was law. A lady in her sixties perhaps paid the most apt tribute to Koussevitzky's personal magnetism by saying: "Even for me, he could be dangerous."

From the musical point of view, Bernstein was fascinated by the contrast between long-memoried Mitropoulos, methodical Reiner, and an unorthodox genius whose system of conducting, while it conformed to no known rules, got results.

One of the classic Koussevitzky stories concerns his erratic beat. "We got together," a player in the orchestra is supposed to have said, "and decided that when his hand passes the third button on his vest, that's the downbeat."

Another time, the musicians took their perplexity to Koussevitzky himself. The reply was a Koussevitzkyism which Bernstein loves to quote:

"Ven my stick touches de air, you play."

"Now, that says nothing," Bernstein observes, "and yet it says everything. When you want an ethereal sound, as at the beginning of the Prelude to *Lohengrin,* a downbeat would be almost too crude. The 'stick touching the air' is really the effect you want."

Koussevitzky had been known to lose his place in the score, and to give wrong cues—which the orchestra placidly ignored. After one such occasion at Carnegie Hall, a baffled critic headed his review: "Koussevitzky Does It With Mirrors."

In a book which Koussevitzky tried, unsuccessfully, to have suppressed, it was hinted that the conductor did not know how to read a full score. This rumor was apparently based on the fact that Koussevitzky had once retained Nicolas Slonimsky, Vengerova's brilliant nephew, as "musical secretary" to save him the drudgery of going through scores submitted for performance.

Musically, Koussevitzky understood quite well what he was about. His shortcoming was that he did not know how to explain it. His mind, unlike Reiner's, was hopelessly non-analytical. But he had an ear, he knew what he wanted, and he screamed until he got it.

"Koussy used to say, 'Eet mus' be more beautiful,'" Bernstein recalls. "Nobody would know what was wrong or why it wasn't beautiful enough already. But they would try again and eventually it *was* more beautiful."

In most orchestras, it is a part of the concertmaster's function to serve as liaison between conductor and orchestra, explaining what the Maestro *really* meant when he said "rallentando." In Richard Burgin, the Boston Symphony Orchestra was fortunate to have a concertmaster of more than ordinary tact and resourcefulness. Some were inclined to give him more than a concertmaster's share of credit for the glories of the B. S. O.

"I was very close to Dr. Koussevitzky," Burgin once said tactfully apropos of this point. He added:

53

"The longer a group plays together, the better its ensemble will be. That is true of anything from a string quartet on up."

This was the B. S. O. secret. It was the orchestra's policy to engage relatively few guest conductors. Through long years of working together, Koussevitzky and the orchestra had arrived at mutual understanding. Each knew what to expect from the other.

This conductor-orchestra relationship fascinated Bernstein, as did nearly everything else about Koussevitzky. The conductor for his part was drawn to the dark, intense, precociously gifted young musician. The warm and enduring friendship which began at Tanglewood in the summer of 1940 ended only with Koussevitzky's death. If Helen Coates had been a sort of musical mother to the confused boy of fourteen, Koussevitzky was a musical father to the harassed musician of twenty-two. Without children of his own, and eager to hand down his store of musical wisdom to a younger generation, Koussevitzky found in Bernstein an ideally receptive audience.

It was in fact upon him that Bernstein came to model most closely his own conducting style, imitating him so successfully as to be dubbed "Koussevitzky in short pants."

In musical circles, word gets around. It was made clear to Bernstein that he could not expect to be a Reiner protégé and a Koussevitzky protégé as well. The budding young conductor was faced with a difficult decision. Should he go back to the Institute for further study with Reiner, or not?

He laid the problem before Koussevitzky. He still treasures the letter which he received in reply. It is a revealing evaluation of one artist by another, in a field where professional jealousy is not unknown.

"If you want to have my advice," Koussevitzky wrote, "pay a great deal of attention to every remark made by Mr. Reiner. He is, as you know, a master technician and holds the best European traditions of musical art."

After a second, final year in Philadelphia, Bernstein received his diploma at the 1941 Curtis commencement. When he returned to Tanglewood that summer, it was with the special status of a Koussevitzky "find." When Koussevitzky discovered talent, he was not reticent about announcing it. Dorothy Maynor and Mario Lanza were two of the singers to whom he said: "Yours is a voice such as is heard only once in a hundred years." In Bernstein's case, Koussevitzky proclaimed the young man's talent to such good effect that Bernstein was soon one of the recognized "sights" of Tanglewood.

Tanglewood is a pleasant place to spend the summer. The old Aspinwall-Tappan estate, which was bequeathed to the Boston Symphony Orchestra,

55

is one of the showplaces of western Massachusetts. For Bernstein, there was the added thrill of "a real orchestra, every week!"

Much later, Bernstein would write concerning this problem, peculiar to the young conductor: "A violinist has a violin and practices on it at home, likewise a piccolo or tuba player. But a conductor needs an instrument which is far too expensive to buy, far too large to house, and far too busy to be at his constant disposition. It is a real problem for a young conductor."

Now, at Tanglewood, that part of the problem was solved. The group which he rehearsed and conducted was the student orchestra, but by no means negligible on that account. These were pretty advanced students, a select group assembled from all parts of the nation. Bernstein had his orchestra, and made the most of it.

Also stimulating were sessions with Aaron Copland, who was now on the Tanglewood faculty. Although Bernstein never formally studied composition with Copland, he often submitted manuscripts for Copland's opinion.

"This is lousy, and this sounds like Scriabin," Copland would say with the frankness of old friendship, "but go home and write some more."

Despite the informality of this arrangement, Copland's style was and still is one of the most important influences in Bernstein's own music.

Koussevitzky was giving Bernstein increasingly important assignments—so much so that rumors began circulating that the young musician was being groomed as Koussevitzky's successor with the Boston Symphony Orchestra.

"Lenyushka," Koussevitzky said one day, "it is time for you to conduct *choeur*."

The *"choeur"* finally selected was *Rio Grande,* a big work in jazz idiom for chorus and orchestra by Constant Lambert, based on a poem of Sacheverell Sitwell. For Bernstein to have tackled the work at all showed temerity; even more so was to attempt it with a student orchestra, chorus, and piano soloist.

The work was to be performed at an evening concert. After the final rehearsal that afternoon, Bernstein was introduced to Tallulah Bankhead, who was playing summer stock in the neighborhood.

"Darling," Miss Bankhead intoned, "I have gone mad over your back muscles. You must come and have dinner with me."

Nothing was further from Bernstein's wishes, with a strenuous performance coming up, than to scintillate at dinner. But Miss Bankhead had a mind of her own. She swept him into her car in his rehearsal clothes—Basque shirt and dungarees —and whisked him off to nearby Stockbridge for refreshments.

Time stood still while they ate, drank and talked, until Bernstein discovered with concern that he was having trouble in focusing his eyes. He asked the time. It was eight o'clock. The concert began at eight-fifteen and *Rio Grande* was second on the program.

With an assist from Miss Bankhead's chauffeur, Bernstein rushed to his apartment, hurried into summer formals and sped to the festival grounds in time to hear the conclusion of the opening number, led by a fellow student-conductor.

Throughout his career, Bernstein has displayed a faculty for rising to the occasion at moments of stress. This was certainly one of them.

The fervor of his conducting communicated itself to the student orchestra and chorus. He fired their imaginations to such good effect that the performance was a huge success. Koussevitzky beamed approbation for his "Lenyushka."

Chapter 4

IN THE AUTUMN OF 1941, Bernstein, although enriched as a musician by his association with Vengerova, Reiner, and Koussevitzky, nevertheless found himself in the same position as upon his graduation from Harvard. He needed a job.

Mitropoulos would have liked to have him in Minneapolis, but the Minneapolis Symphony budget did not provide for an assistant conductor.

When he heard that Bernstein was planning another descent upon New York, Koussevitzky advised him to stay in Boston. The Mexican composer-conductor Carlos Chavez was to make a guest appearance with the B. S. O. "Lenyushka" could be the soloist in Chavez's new piano concerto. The fee from this performance, plus whatever he could earn from musical odd jobs around Boston, would

59

keep him going until Tanglewood reopened the following summer.

Bernstein readily agreed. A tedious, frustrating winter was the result.

Bernstein's principal disappointment was that the Chavez performance did not come off. The Boston Symphony Orchestra was at this time the last major non-union orchestra in the country. President James C. Petrillo of the American Federation of Musicians established a virtual blockade of the orchestra with his decree that no member of the union might perform with the B. S. O. This eliminated both Bernstein and Chavez.

A more searching test of trade-union loyalty could scarcely be imagined; but Bernstein remained faithful to the A. F. of M.

Meanwhile, he opened a piano studio on Huntington Avenue. "I did the usual things," he says. "I sent out announcements, and waited for results. Nobody came. *Nobody!*"

One reason was that he opened his studio two days before December 7, 1941. After the attack on Pearl Harbor, Americans had other things than piano study on their minds.

Once again, Bernstein's father put pressure on him to enter the family business. Bernstein resisted as stubbornly as ever. He played a few benefit concerts and organized musical events at the Institute of Modern Art, including a performance of Copland's opera for students, *The Second Hurricane*.

He felt himself to be hopelessly out of the mainstream of events, musically and otherwise. His draft board, after reviewing his history of asthma, had declined his services with thanks.

With so much time on his hands, Bernstein set about writing a Sonata for Clarinet and Piano. It had its first performance at the Institute of Modern Art on April 21, 1942. David Glazer was the clarinetist, with the composer at the piano. Bernstein would play the work in New York the following season, with David Oppenheim as the clarinetist. The work also had a performance in Philadelphia by Stanley Drucker, then a student at the Curtis Institute and now solo clarinetist of the New York Philharmonic.

Leaving out of account such early efforts as the "Russo-Gypsy War," the Sonatina for Piano, and the Aristophanes music, the Clarinet Sonata may be regarded as Bernstein's Opus 1. As is often the case with an Opus 1, the work is somewhat diffident and tentative when considered in terms of the composer's later, more fully evolved style. It is a rather stiffly correct work reflecting, among other things, the composer's new-found interest in the style of Paul Hindemith.

But it is hard to write convincingly in the Hindemith idiom unless one shares Hindemith's traditionalist point of view, his Central European musical orientation, and his fondness for contrapuntal elaboration of musical ideas. Whether or not Bernstein was consciously aware of this fact, it would probably now be difficult even for him to say. In any case, his musical intuition led him to other fields. The abstractions of sonata form were not quite his dish of tea. The Clarinet Sonata is the one major work by Bernstein which does not incorporate a text, a literary allusion, or a programmatic element of some sort.

If not typical of his more fully evolved style, however, the sonata is by no means a negligible work, for it reflects the high quality of Bernstein's imagination and training. It made clear that he was a composer who had something to say and the technique with which to say it.

The first of his works to receive other than student performance, the sonata was also the first to be published. Witmark brought it out in 1942— a fact which was to have an odd, unexpected sequel seventeen years later.

Aside from performance and publication of his sonata, 1941-42 was a difficult, unsettling winter, brightened occasionally by such things as the Boston tryout of a musical, *My Dear Public*. Betty Comden and Adolph Green of The Revuers were both in the cast. On opening night, they invited Bernstein to a party at the Ritz-Carlton. Bernstein of course gravitated to the piano, where his playing impressed, among others, Irving Caesar, writer of music and lyrics for the show.

After the winter of his discontent, Bernstein was glad to escape to the green lawns of Tanglewood. His pleasure at returning was given a bittersweet tinge by the knowledge that with the end of the 1942 summer concert series, Tanglewood was to be suspended "for the duration." It would be four years before the eight-thirty bell again rang to summon listeners to a concert.

By summer's end, Bernstein had made a crucial decision. Boston, like Philadelphia, was for an unknown musician a hard place in which to do business, and for much the same reason. Musical activity there consisted of the glorious orchestra and not very much else. Eventually, the battle would have to be fought in New York; why postpone it?

So reasoning, Bernstein took the plunge. The ensuing period he remembers as "Bernstein's Valley Forge."

Bernstein lived in an eight-dollar-a-week room, worked when he could, and tried not to think about his mother's cooking. His first months in New York made the previous winter in Boston seem, in retrospect, "just about heaven." He played for ballet classes, gave lessons—"even *voice* lessons," he recalls, wincing. He played three concerts for

63

the troops at Fort Dix, receiving an enthusiastic response but, of course, no pay. Such things were part of the war effort.

Bernstein at this time skipped more than one meal, and was frequently behind in his rent. His morale sank to its lowest level. He was oppressed by the chilling thought that he had no talent, that he would never make it as a musician, and would have been better off to heed his father's advice.

As he had done in 1939, Bernstein made the rounds of music publishers and concert managers, looking for a way to enter the musical world. This time, he was better equipped. A letter from Fritz Reiner attested his "extraordinary gifts." Another from Koussevitzky introduced him as a conductor "of outstanding talent, in whose brilliant future I have great faith." The letters secured for him polite interviews but no jobs.

Bernstein's slim pickings continued through the fall. Then, as has happened throughout his career, an earlier, chance encounter set in motion an unexpected train of events.

In December, he met Irving Caesar, who remembered him perfectly from the Boston party for *My Dear Public*. When Caesar had sung some of his own songs, Bernstein had played for him, improvising accompaniments in a way that reminded Caesar of the late George Gershwin.

Now, learning that Bernstein was finding the

going difficult, Caesar was profoundly shocked.

"What!" he exclaimed. "You, a genius, starving?"

Bernstein explained that his wants were modest. All he needed was ten dollars a week to enable him to stay in New York.

"Ten dollars a week, for a genius?" Caesar said. "I'll get you fifty!"

Caesar got on the phone to Herman Starr of Harms, Inc., now part of Music Publishers Holding Corp. but at that time a subsidiary of Warner Brothers.

"There is a boy here who looks a little like George and plays like George," Caesar told Starr. "I don't know if he writes like George. I want you to pay him fifty dollars a week on my say-so. If he only comes up to your house every Friday night and plays the piano, he is worth fifty dollars of Harry Warner's money."

Starr scaled down the fee to twenty-five dollars per week, a sum on which in those days a single man of frugal habits could live, after a fashion, in New York.

Bernstein was quick and adaptable, with an ear and a thorough knowledge of music. Harms, Inc. soon had him busy at a variety of musical odd jobs. One of the most important was that of putting musical improvisations down on paper.

A great deal of the jazz being recorded in those days consisted of performances improvised on the

65

spot for the standard going rate of one hundred dollars and a bottle of gin per side. In *We Called it Music,* Eddie Condon has amusingly described the easygoing manner in which some of these performances were arranged. To rehearse in advance was an idea which did not occur to any of the players. Repertoire was usually decided in a taxi on the way to the recording studio.

Obviously, under such conditions some recordings were bound to be sour. But there were times when everything clicked into place, players were in the mood, and their playing achieved results worth imitating.

In such a case, it was worth Harms, Inc.'s while to publish the improvisation. This required a keen-eared musician who, by listening to the record, could tell what note each of the instruments was playing, and write them down in the musical shorthand of staff notation—all in the shortest possible time. In Tin Pan Alley, the life span of a tune is proverbially short. A measure of a publishing firm's vitality is whether it can "turn on a dime."

Caught up in the staccato rhythms of jazz publishing, and bringing his highly disciplined musical intelligence to bear on technical problems which, in the early stages at least, were new and interesting, Bernstein nevertheless felt his arrangements, band transcriptions, and so on to be hack work. He

66

signed them with the pseudonym "Lenny Amber." (*Bernstein* in German means amber stone.)

As an antidote, Bernstein played chamber music with clarinetist David Oppenheim, who later became director of artists and repertoire for Columbia Records. They made several broadcasts over station WNYC, one of the works performed being the Clarinet Sonata, which was dedicated to Oppenheim.

As still another antidote, Bernstein in the final days of 1942 was up to his eyebrows in a big new work, a symphony for mezzo-soprano and orchestra employing a text from the Lamentations of Jeremiah which he planned to enter in a contest sponsored by the New England Conservatory of Music. Deadline for the submission of scores was December 31.

Bernstein spent precious time making up his mind whether or not to enter the contest. Having decided, he spent more time planning what sort of a work to enter. By the time the "Jeremiah" Symphony was fully sketched, there were exactly ten days left in which to complete the orchestration and prepare a legible full score.

Then began one of those marathon performances which were to characterize Bernstein's early years. Working day and night, and keeping himself awake with large quantities of black coffee — he had not discovered benzedrine — Bernstein pushed the score to completion. Sister Shirley and friends lent a hand with the copying.

The score was ready in time, but with not much to spare. Bernstein had cut it so fine that he dared not trust the mails. Instead, he took the train to Boston and personally delivered the manuscript to the New England Conservatory. Then he returned to New York and went to bed for a week.

It is regrettable that such energy and zeal did not win the prize. Such, however, was the case— although in 1944 the score won an award from the Music Critics Circle of New York. (And, seventeen years later, the "Jeremiah" Symphony was to be part of a tribute to Bernstein without precedent in New York music history.)

Another bitter pill was that Koussevitzky, on examining the score, told Bernstein he did not like it.

No one could accuse Koussevitzky of being unreceptive either to new music or to Bernstein. Was his judgment of the piece unduly severe? Perhaps. On the other hand, the most fervent Bernstein admirer would hardly deny that the "Jeremiah" Symphony has flaws, some the consequence of the haste with which it was written. Its obvious merits are vividness and originality. It is the work of an imaginative musician with a fresh point of view. Its obvious shortcoming is lack of sure-handed technical proficiency. While its best moments are fine and striking, the work as a whole is uneven. It does not quite hang together.

When the work was performed; many listeners felt the final movement for voice and orchestra to be almost an interpolation, having little relation to what had gone before. Olin Downes aptly described it as an "accompanied vocal monologue" rather than a movement genuinely symphonic in nature.

And this in fact is what it was. In the summer of 1939, Bernstein had begun sketching a work for mezzo-soprano and orchestra on the text from Lamentations. This was, among other things, the reflection of a family tradition of Talmudic scholarship. His great-grandfather, although he made his living as a blacksmith, had been an ordained and practicing rabbi. The next two generations produced Talmudists also. And young Leonard, on the occasion of his graduation in *bar mitzvah* ceremonies at Temple Mishkan Tefila in Boston, had distinguished himself by composing what his family still regards as a brilliant speech in Hebrew.

As a compliment to his father, who spoke the Ashkenazic dialect of Hebrew, Bernstein used the Ashkenazic text for his "Jeremiah." Later, when the work was performed in Israel, he adapted it to the Sephardic dialect preferred there.

Having sketched his "Jeremiah" music, Bernstein laid it aside. Three years later, with time running out for the New England Conservatory's deadline, it occurred to him that the "Jeremiah" music could serve as the final movement of his symphony.

It could and did; but in the nature of things it could not sound like an integrated movement developing logically from the previous two. Also it seems to be a law of the creative process that returning to an unfinished or unsatisfactory earlier work is difficult. Verdi's long and fruitless tinkerings with *Don Carlo* and *Simon Boccanegra* are examples. And H. L. Mencken, offered the chance to revise one of his earlier books, found he could not do it. He was no longer the same writer; to meddle with the book would only spoil it.

The artist evolves and changes; his style matures; his thought and general cast of mind are altered. Even three years can be a long time when, as with the gestation period of Bernstein's "Jeremiah" music, they span a transit through the Curtis Institute and the beginnings of an association with Koussevitzky.

Bernstein was, naturally, made unhappy by the reception of his work as fragmentary, and in particular by the suggestion that he had merely tacked on an earlier piece as a conclusion.

"There was much more serious thought given to the work than this implies," Bernstein told this writer. "Every composer draws on earlier material without necessarily producing an 'integrated' work."

70

In any event, the "Jeremiah" Symphony represented a turn toward what time has shown to be the true orientation of Bernstein's musical thought —music based upon or in some way bound up with a literary text, allusion, or idea. It was an orientation which would eventually lead him to the theater.

The idea man, like Liszt, Berlioz, or Richard Strauss, is a recognized musical type. There is sometimes a tendency to ascribe greater pride of place to the musical abstractionist, the composer of symphonies and sonatas having no external point of reference. Why this should be so is not clear. The ability to write a successful opera, for example, is a skill which is extremely rare; that is why it is so highly rewarded. Composers who have died rich have been almost without exception those who wrote for the stage.

If Koussevitzky did not care for Bernstein's "Jeremiah," Reiner was more impressed. He invited Bernstein to make his debut with the Pittsburgh Symphony, conducting his own work, the following season.

("And so did Koussevitzky," Bernstein reminded the writer, "directly after the Pittsburgh première.")

For the rest of the winter of 1942-43, Bernstein plugged away at arrangements for Harms, Inc. Early the next summer, he received a call from

Koussevitzky. Although the war had made it impossible to hold the Berkshire Festival in 1943, Koussevitzky was, as usual, spending the summer at his hilltop estate overlooking the festival grounds. He was to give a lecture for the benefit of the Red Cross in Lenox, and wanted to make it a lecture-recital with Bernstein at the piano. Would Bernstein help out?

To Bernstein, sweltering in Manhattan heat and gasping with asthma, the thought of Koussevitzky's breezy terrace was irresistible. He obtained a leave of absence from Harms, Inc. and headed for Massachusetts.

In Boston, he paid a call at his draft board. The wheezing musician was again turned down. As Bernstein was leaving, the Army Medical Corps major who had marked his papers 4-F handed him a pamphlet. It was a treatise by the major on asthma.

Boston was hot, too. Bernstein telephoned Miss Coates to invite her to join him and Shirley in a trip to Lenox, where he was to give a series of performances. (The original lecture-recital had now been expanded to three events, including a joint recital by Bernstein and mezzo-soprano Jennie Tourel.)

Miss Coates said she would love to go, and on a Saturday morning in August all three took the train to the Berkshires.

On their arrival, Bernstein received from Koussevitzky a piece of unexpected news. Artur Rodzinski wanted to see him.

Rodzinski, who had just taken over the direction of the New York Philharmonic, and who would storm out of that directorship, as he had stormed out of a number of others, had for some time been a summer resident of the Berkshires. Goats' milk from his farm near Stockbridge went daily to metropolitan distribution points, including the drugstore of the RCA Building in Radio City.

In previous summers, Rodzinski had attended Berkshire Festival concerts regularly, and had seen Bernstein at work. In the back of his mind, Rodzinski had been mulling over the idea of engaging an assistant to help him prepare the Philharmonic's programs. Such an assistant would be preferably one who was young, bright, musical, and a hard worker. The specifications fitted Bernstein like a glove.

All this was of course unknown to Bernstein when he called Rodzinski. He received an invitation to come to Stockbridge at noon the next day.

Rodzinski did not ask Bernstein to play for him, or to go through a score. Instead, he seated the wheezing musician by a rick of new-mown hay, and talked. A devout Buchmanite, Rodzinski believed in the power of divine inspiration, and on this occasion appeared to be watching for a sign from heaven.

About an hour later, Rodzinski's car delivered

Bernstein to his hotel. Shirley and Miss Coates were on the veranda, reading the Sunday papers.

Bernstein said casually: "Meet the new assistant conductor of the New York Philharmonic."

It was as simple as that.

In the evening, the new assistant conductor played for Jennie Tourel's recital, a feature of which was the first performance of Bernstein's new song cycle, "I Hate Music." Koussevitzky, who did not care very much for the songs, had been dubious about including them in the program. As a compromise, he had suggested that Miss Tourel sing them as an encore.

She did, and they made an immediate hit.

The date of this eventful Sunday was August 25th. All things considered, the new assistant conductor of the Philharmonic must have reflected, it was not a bad way of celebrating one's twenty-fifth birthday.

A few days later, back in Boston, Helen Coates received a newspaper clipping which she has carefully preserved ever since. It was a news item from the New York *Times* announcing Bernstein's appointment as assistant conductor of the Philharmonic. On the margin was a note in Bernstein's handwriting:

"Here we go! Love, Lenny."

Chapter 5

IN THE AUTUMN OF 1943, Bernstein, exchanging his eight-dollar-a-week room for a hundred-dollar-a-month studio at Carnegie Hall, set out to master his new duties as assistant conductor of the New York Philharmonic.

These duties, in practice, vary from orchestra to orchestra. Although the assistant conductor's name appears on the program in larger type than that of the concertmaster, his principal function may prove to be that of bringing coffee and sandwiches to the conductor at rehearsal.

Said to hold true for all situations, however, is a somewhat cynical maxim: the more talent an assistant conductor has, the less opportunity he will find to display it.

An assistant conductorship can in fact be a dead

end street. For an assistant to assume command of an orchestra upon the departure or demise of its conductor is an event of such rarity that one is hard put to recall an instance.

What usually happens instead is that vacancies are filled in exactly the same way as the pulpit of a fashionable parish. Invitations are tendered to men who have made a good showing elsewhere. The man who accepts leaves a vacancy at his former post, which on being filled creates another vacancy somewhere else, and so on, with repercussions felt throughout the whole conductorial chessboard. Assistants, meanwhile, sit out this game of musical chairs pretty much where they were before.

When Bernstein took the Philharmonic post, he was well aware of the hazards of assistant conductorship. But he was young and it was an opportunity to acquaint himself with a famous orchestra, and to observe at work bluff, blustery Rodzinski, a conductorial personality different from any he had known before.

Dutifully, Bernstein attended rehearsals, making it clear that he was available if needed. In his free time, he rounded out his 1943 creative output by composing a piano suite, "Seven Anniversaries."

Each of its seven sections was intended as a musical characterization of a person close to Bernstein—his sister Shirley, Serge and Natalie Kous-

76

sevitzky, his fellow-composers Aaron Copland, Paul Bowles, and William Schuman, and Alfred Eisner, a Harvard roommate. Bernstein played the first performance of the suite at a benefit concert at the Boston Opera House on May 14, 1944. On October 13, the Canadian pianist Gordon Manley gave "Seven Anniversaries" its New York première at Town Hall.

The possibilities of the "musical portrait" had already been explored by Virgil Thomson and "les six français." What made Bernstein's suite interesting was not its novelty but the soundness of its construction and the composer's thorough grasp of what would or would not "go," pianistically speaking.

Bernstein's musical idiom was severely contemporary; it appeared that his admiration for Hindemith was still strong. There was also a hint of what would be marked in his later output—great fluency in adapting the materials of jazz to his musical purpose.

Jazz can be a headache for the contemporary composer. Some musicians have no feeling for it whatsoever. On the other hand, jazz is so peculiarly and uniquely an American contribution to the vocabulary of music that a composer may write in a jazz idiom from a sense of duty, feeling that as an American composer he ought to be writing "American music," whatever that may be. In such

77

a case, the jazzy passages often turn out to be stiff and self-conscious, wholly lacking in that easy spontaneity which is a jazz attribute.

For Bernstein, jazz had no terrors. He had rounded out his early dance band apprenticeship by working in a Tin Pan Alley tunesmithy. His sure-handedness with jazz was that of a professional. He knew the medium.

With "Seven Anniversaries," Bernstein's creative work for 1943 was done. The Philharmonic season was hardly a month old when it became clear that his name would not appear season after season just above the roster of first violins.

During the second week in November, Bruno Walter was guest conductor of the Philharmonic. He was scheduled to lead the concerts of Thursday evening, Friday afternoon, and Sunday afternoon, November 11, 12, and 14.

The Thursday evening concert went smoothly. On Friday afternoon, Walter told Bruno Zirato, the orchestra's associate manager, after the concert: "Bruno, I don't feel well. I think I have the damn flu."

On Saturday morning, Walter called Zirato again. He was running a temperature, the conductor reported. He did not think he could make it on Sunday afternoon.

Zirato had a sinking feeling. Rodzinski having, as he supposed, finished his stint with the orchestra, was out of town, vacationing in Stockbridge. He relayed the news to Bernstein.

"All right," Bernstein replied. "I was at the rehearsals all week, but I'd like to look at the markings in Dr. Walter's scores. Can I have them?"

Much reassured by Bernstein's cool reply, Zirato promised to send up the scores immediately.

The truth of the matter was that Bernstein did not for a moment believe he would actually conduct the performance. The situation of the unknown young assistant conductor coming forward to save the day was too much like a movie plot to be believable.

Uppermost in Bernstein's mind, moreover, was an event which was to take place at Town Hall that night—the New York recital debut of Jennie Tourel. Miss Tourel had already sung at the Metropolitan, winning special praise for her vivid portrayal of Carmen. As a recitalist, however, she was an unknown quantity, hence lovers of vocalism turned out in house-filling numbers.

Among the audience were Bernstein and his parents. Mr. and Mrs. Bernstein had made the trip from Boston because the recital was his most important appearance thus far as a composer. His "I Hate Music" cycle was the final group on Miss Tourel's program.

The cycle of "kid songs" was perhaps a bit

flippant to bear the name of a Philharmonic assistant conductor, since among other things the cycle
gently poked fun at the solemnities of the concert
hall. The performer represents a ten-year-old girl
who sings:

> Music is a lot of folks in a big dark hall where
> they really don't want to be at all;
> With a lot of chairs, and a lot of airs, and a
> lot of furs and diamonds;
> Music is silly! I hate music!
> But I like to sing!

This tickled the audience greatly. The recital
as a whole was such a success that it pleased Noel
Straus, the immensely learned, immensely finicky
New York *Times* critic who had heard Amalia
Materna in 1893 and every important singer,
without exception, since.

He praised Bernstein's songs as "amusing,"
though pointing out that they appeared to show
the influence of Moussorgsky's "Nursery" cycle.
(As a matter of fact, Bernstein at that point had
never heard the Moussorgsky songs.)

Bernstein said good night to his family, who
were spending the night at the Hotel Barbizon,
intending to return to Boston the next day.

He then joined a convivial party at Miss Tourel's
apartment, where he celebrated by drinking Scotch
highballs and sharing with Miss Tourel congratu-
lations on the success of the recital. Time spent

in this way passed so pleasantly that he did not get back to his studio until four A.M.

At eight o'clock, he was awakened by a call from Zirato.

"Take the scores and go see Maestro Walter," said Zirato. "He can't conduct today."

"Oh, my God," was Bernstein's reply. He had not had very much sleep.

Nevertheless, he hauled himself out of bed, dressed, and went immediately to Walter's hotel on Fifth Avenue. He found the older conductor in bed, wrapped in blankets and shivering.

With scores in hand, Bernstein and Walter went over the afternoon's music—Schumann's "Manfred" Overture, Strauss's *Don Quixote,* a new work by Miklós Rózsa entitled *Theme, Variations and Finale,* and the Prelude to *Die Meistersinger.*

In a sense, Bernstein's task was more difficult than if he had been a regularly scheduled guest conductor. While the impact of a guest conductor on an orchestra is not so great as some listeners suppose—it would be folly in a brief guest engagement to attempt radically new interpretations of works which the orchestra already plays—nevertheless within broad areas of tempo, phrasing, and dynamics, there is latitude for individuality. When a guest conductor has ended his engagement, the librarian's first task is to erase the musicians' pencil markings in the orchestra parts.

But in this case the pencil marks were from Bruno Walter's rehearsals. The program had been rehearsed all week and played in public twice. It was no time for rugged individualism; Bernstein had no choice but to do the music as nearly in Bruno Walter's way as was possible.

At eleven o'clock, Bernstein called his father at the Barbizon.

"Do you remember me telling you Friday that you would have to wait ten years to see me conduct the Philharmonic?"

"Yes."

"I made a slight miscalculation," Bernstein said. "You're going to see me this afternoon."

Although his debut did not find Bernstein wholly unprepared, it did catch him without the striped trousers and formal coat which are standard attire for an afternoon musical event. He donned his nearest equivalent, a dark gray flannel suit, and took the elevator down to Fifty-seventh Street.

By now the strain was beginning to tell. In order to calm his jumpy nerves he went into a drugstore for coffee.

"What's the matter?" asked the pharmacist, who knew him. "You look terrible."

"I have to conduct this afternoon."

"Wait a minute." Rummaging in a drawer, the pharmacist produced a blue pill and a white pill. "Take these new pills. The phenobarbital will quiet your nerves and the benzedrine will give you energy."

Bernstein slipped the pills into his pocket, completely forgetting about them until he was in the wings, ready to make his entrance. Then, with what he later described as a "grand and heroic gesture," he dashed them to the stage.

At concert time, Zirato went out to announce the change of conductors. After explaining that Dr. Walter was ill, Zirato added: "We are now going to witness the debut of a full-fledged American conductor, born and entirely trained in this country."

A polite, perfunctory spatter of applause greeted Bernstein as he mounted the podium and raised his arm for the down-beat.

When he stepped down again two hours later, there was a tumultuous standing ovation, heard all over the nation via the Sunday afternoon Philharmonic broadcast.

In two hours, he had become famous.

Besides its musical importance, this was a human interest story of the sort which everybody loves. The press made the most of it. The *Times* ran Olin Downes's review on page one, with, for good measure, an editorial, "A Story Old, Yet Ever New." The Horatio Alger formula was timeless.

Downes gave high praise to the interesting new talent. The "Manfred" Overture had been lively, if at times somewhat over-driven. The Rózsa piece had been interpreted for what it was worth, which was not very much. The *Meistersinger* Prelude had been "splendid," and *Don Quixote* well done, if not quite up to Bruno Walter level.

Players in the orchestra sometimes see things in a different light from listeners out front. To a Philharmonic man who took part in the historic performance, *Don Quixote* was Bernstein's most brilliant achievement of the afternoon.

"There are some things where all we need is a pay check and a down-beat," he said. "*Don Quixote* isn't like that at all. It's a tricky score. There are plenty of places where a green conductor can get into trouble. That Sunday, it was Bernstein who held the performance together. He had the orchestra following him. It was magnificent."

Bernstein, in short, had been much more than adequate. An audience ready to overlook short-comings because of the emergency nature of his debut had found little to forgive and much to praise. When his big opportunity came, Bernstein was ready.

This appears to be the great secret of a performing career. In the course of time, everyone is likely to have a certain number of opportunities, just as everyone is likely to hold at least a few good hands in an evening of bridge. The great thing is to be ready when opportunity comes. The next great thing is to know one is ready and have assurance one can bring off the performance successfully. The final great thing is to succeed.

The Philharmonic concert appears to have marked Bernstein's permanent, lifelong farewell to privacy. Next day, his studio was jammed with reporters, and spent flashbulbs made walking perilous. This is a state of affairs with which he has lived fairly constantly ever since.

But Bernstein had little time to worry about such things. To say his career was expanding is an understatement. It was soaring upward like a string of booster rockets, in a series of explosions each more spectacular than the last, and with no ceiling in sight.

The sheer bulk and scope of his activities in his first year before the public led one friend to nominate Bernstein "musical decathlon champion of the world."

Two weeks after his Philharmonic debut, Bernstein led the orchestra in Bloch's "Three Jewish Poems," this time with rehearsals. And on December 16, as if to prove lightning could strike twice, Bernstein filled in at short notice for the ailing Howard Barlow, conducting with success a difficult program which included the Brahms *Haydn Variations, Paris* by Delius and the Beethoven Violin Concerto, with Albert Spalding as soloist.

With the wisdom of hindsight, it appears that

Virgil Thomson's comment on this concert was a balanced judgment on Bernstein's qualities at this time, as well as a sound prophecy.

For a second time this season, [Thomson wrote] epidemic influenza has given us a Philharmonic concert conducted by the excellent Leonard Bernstein. In previous years guest conductors didn't fall ill. Maybe it is the knowledge that Mr. Bernstein will meet all such emergencies more than capably that enables them nowadays to give in. In any case, last night's concert was a lovely one so far as Mr. Bernstein and the orchestra were concerned. Its only weakness was the conductor's inability (he is too young and too straightforward to be skillful yet at this tactical problem) to conceal the essential secondrateness of Delius' music and of Albert Spalding's violin playing.

I suspect that Mr. Bernstein's striking quality as a conductor is largely due to his rhythmic understanding. His enlightenment in this regard is superior to that of any of the contemporary great, saving only Beecham. He does not draw a big orchestral tone. He calls forth well the melody parts and the basses. And he outlines the architecture of a piece better than most. But he does not always keep the horns and other filling parts at adequate supporting level for the full rendering of his architectural design. That will come with more experience; it is a thing that can be learned. Rhythm and pitch cannot be learned; they can be perfected but not learned. You have them basically or not. Mr. Bernstein has them, and that is why his work gives one a great confidence. His real ability to handle serious music as if it belonged to him (and he to it) makes one certain inside that here is no flash-in-the-pan.

86

Heady praise, arriving at a welcome time for a young conductor just beginning to establish himself. Bernstein's relations with the press would not always be this serene; many a comment from the devastating *Herald Tribune* critic in particular would make him wince in the future.

Even so, there was no trace of condescension or a pat-the-young-man-on-the-head attitude; it was a serious, thoughtful evaluation of one musician by another. All performers, of whatever kind, love to be taken seriously, at least in the early stages of their careers, and Bernstein was no exception.

In January, Bernstein flew to Pittsburgh to conduct the world première of his "Jeremiah" Symphony, with Miss Tourel as soloist. Soloist, guest conductor, and new work all were acclaimed. Later, following its first New York performance, also with Miss Tourel, "Jeremiah," despite its failure to finish in the money in the contest for which it was written, would receive the 1944 orchestral award of the Music Critics Circle of New York.

The Pittsburgh engagement was the beginning of a guest conducting marathon. Before the year was out, Bernstein would travel 50,000 miles and conduct eighty-nine concerts with orchestras all over the country.

In February, the Philharmonic announced that Bernstein's contract as assistant conductor was not being renewed. Instead, he was being invited back next season as a full-fledged guest conductor.

Everybody was happy but Rodzinski, who somewhat gloweringly let it be known that the less he saw of his quondam assistant conductor, the happier he would be. Bernstein had stepped out of his frame of reference; such things were not supposed to happen to assistant conductors.

Chapter 6

*I*N 1944, THE AMERICAN BALLET THEATER had launched the wonderfully creative era during which it handed out commissions by the fistful to composers and choreographers, in the process building a repertoire which for color, freshness, and variety was not rivaled by any native ballet company.

Bernstein was drawn into the Ballet Theater circle through his friendship with Jerome Robbins, a dancer-choreographer as young, talented, and eager-beaver as Bernstein himself. Robbins had an idea for a ballet, for which he wanted Bernstein to write the music. Bernstein said he would love to. The fact that Robbins would be on tour with Ballet Theater during the early months of 1944 and that Bernstein would be guest-conducting at an average rate of one concert every four days, did not strike either of them as appalling, even though the new ballet was planned for performance during Ballet Theater's April season in New York.

Few ballet scores can have been written under greater difficulty than *Fancy Free,* as the new work was called. Bernstein was conducting; Robbins, with whose choreographic plans Bernstein's music had naturally to be co-ordinated, was touring; and a further complication was that Oliver Smith, the designer, was in Mexico.

The three kept in touch by telegram and telephone. As each section of the music was completed, Bernstein would record it and ship the recording to wherever Robbins and Ballet Theater happened to be appearing. Back by telegram or telephone would come Robbins's comments and suggested changes.

In this roundabout fashion, somewhat to the surprise of all concerned, *Fancy Free* was completed in time for performance during Ballet Theater's spring season at the Metropolitan Opera House. The first performance took place on April 18, 1944, with Bernstein conducting.

Fancy Free has been well described in Robbins's own words:

With the sound of a juke box, the curtain rises on a street corner with a lamp post, a side street bar, and New York skyscrapers pricked out with a crazy pattern of lights, making a dizzying background. Three sailors explode on the stage; they are on shore leave in the city and on the prowl for girls. The tale of how they meet first one, then a second girl, and how they fight over them, lose them and in the end take off after still a third, is the story of the ballet.

Fancy Free was an immediate success. It was bright, fresh, and topical. Bernstein's lively, unselfconsciously jazzy score was attuned to the rhythm and tempo of the times. An America at war wanted distraction from the stress and anxieties of its colossal world-wide war effort, and *Fancy Free* was it.

So insistent was the demand for tickets to *Fancy Free* that the Ballet Theater season was extended two weeks beyond its scheduled closing; instead of seven performances of *Fancy Free*, Bernstein led nineteen. Altogether, *Fancy Free* was danced one hundred and sixty-one times during its first season.

Inevitably, the next question was: if *Fancy Free* was so solid a hit in ballet form, would it not make an equal success if expanded into a musical? Bernstein discussed the point with Robbins, with Betty Comden and Adolph Green, and with director George Abbott. All agreed the answer was Yes.

Work on the musical began under picturesque circumstances. In the summer of 1944, Bernstein was to undergo an operation for a deviated septum, and Green was to have his tonsils out. They arranged to have their operations scheduled at the same time, and shared a hospital room.

91

Friends remember the Bernstein-Green convalescence as sounding more like a cocktail party than a sickroom, with radios blaring, arguments going over gin rummy games and bits of *On the Town* being sung full-voice by composer and lyricists.

Once they were out of the hospital, the collaborators worked to such good effect that the musical was ready to open on December 26. It was obvious from the start that it would be a sensational hit. Even before it went into rehearsal, the film rights were sold to M-G-M for more than $100,000. *On the Town* had a Broadway run of four hundred and sixty-three performances, and when revived fifteen years later it made some of the 1959 musicals appear anemic by comparison.

What gave *On the Town* its particular, unique appeal? It had originality, youthful verve, and sprightly tunes; but there were other musicals which could say as much.

Bernstein's special contribution was a degree of musical sophistication not always associated with the Broadway theater. The man who could employ jazz idioms for abstract musical purposes could also use the devices of symphonic rhetoric to make a theatrical point. A born showman, with the theater in his blood, Bernstein was also a well-trained musician with the whole vocabulary of post-romantic symphonic practice at his finger tips. The musical was more than a succession of "numbers" strung like clothespins on a more or less tenuous story-line; it was a fused, musically integrated, well-knit whole.

It was a far cry from the musicals which, as Bernstein himself was later to point out in an engaging essay, were essentially Americanized forms of the European operetta. In the latter, with a comedian like Bert Lahr or Bobby Clark to tell jokes, and with pretty voices to sing the pretty tunes, everything else was cheerfully accepted as mere filler. The operetta took place in a remote, impossibly glamorous locale; the musical was of here and now, an up-to-date and sometimes irreverent commentary on the passing scene. *On the Town* could trace its line of descent through *Of Thee I Sing!* rather than *Naughty Marietta*.

The Gershwin musical, a witty, delicious satire of national foibles, also could boast a number of memorable Gershwin tunes. *On the Town* had the wit and satire; did it also have the tunes?

On this particular point, Bernstein would become increasingly touchy as the years and musicals increased. Later on, one of his delightful "Imaginary Conversations," in his book *The Joy of Music,* would describe a publisher's representative who asked, in effect, "Why Don't You Run Upstairs and Write a Nice Gershwin Tune?"

"Your songs are simply too arty, that's all," the

publisher's man says. "You try too hard to make them what you would call 'interesting.' That's not for the public, you know. A special little dissonant effect in the bass may make *you* happy, and maybe some of your highbrow friends, but it doesn't help to make a hit. You're too wrapped up in unusual chords and odd skips in the tune and screwy forms; that's all only an amusing game you play with yourself. George [Gershwin] didn't worry about all that. He wrote tunes, dozens of them, simple tunes that the world could sing and remember and want to sing again. He wrote for people, not for critics. You just have to learn how to be simple, my boy."

"You think it's so simple to be simple?" the imaginary Bernstein retorts. "Not at all. I've tried hard for years. After all, this isn't the first time I'm hearing this lecture. A few weeks ago a serious composer-friend and I were talking about all this, and we got boiling mad about it. Why shouldn't we be able to come up with a hit, we said, if the standard is as low as it seems to be? We decided that all we had to do was put ourselves into the mental state of an idiot and write a ridiculous hillbilly tune. So we went to work with a will, vowing to make thousands by simply being simple-minded. We worked for an hour and then gave up in hysterical despair. Impossible. We found ourselves 'being personal' and 'expressing ourselves'; and try as we might we couldn't seem to boil any music down to the bare, feeble-minded level we had set ourselves. I remember that at one point we were trying like two children, one note at a time, to make a tune that didn't even require any harmony, it would be that obvious. Impossible. It was a revealing experiment, I must say, even though it left us with a slightly doomed feeling."

Frustrating, indeed. Bernstein had written a symphony before he even attempted a popular song. That one should be capable of the complexities of a "Jeremiah," but unable to create one of those deceptively simple tunes which people like to whistle must have been galling indeed.

Bernstein, however, was handicapped, perhaps without realizing it, to the extent that he shared the attitude of the musical circle of which he is at least a part-time member. On this particular point, the modern composer is in a box of his own devising. The once clearly understood terms "tune" and "melody" have become fogged through insistence that whatever the composer states to be a melody *is* a melody. Many composers are in fact rather skeptical of melody; one does not write catchpenny tunes to please the crowd. There is superb (and possibly unconscious) hauteur in Bernstein's endeavor to "boil music down to bare, feeble-minded level." It is true that simplicity is the rule, but not any simple succession of tones will do. There is more to it than that. The ability to invent tunes of distinction is a rare and wonderful gift.

But if it was not clear that Bernstein possessed it to the same degree as a Gershwin, Jerome Kern, or Cole Porter, *On the Town* made clear that the cumulative impact of his music was bracing, and sent listeners out ready to urge their friends to see the show.

Olin Downes summed it up well in describing *On the Town* as a "brilliant, swift-paced affair which brings a new style, technique and tempo to a conglomerate and extremely diverting satire on New York City."

The golden year of 1944 had still another accolade in store for Bernstein. The United States Junior Chamber of Commerce voted him, along with John Hersey, Hal Boyle, and Nelson A. Rockefeller, one of the "Ten Outstanding Young Men of 1944."

Chapter 7

IN HORSE-PLAYING CIRCLES, there is a "theory of
ever-changing cycles," based on the universal tendency to gang up on the favorite. In his own field,
Bernstein found something of the same sort. His
fame was making him a prominent target for
criticism.

Some of it was directed at his conducting
technique, and took such predictable form that
Bernstein once declared "acrobatic" and "choreographic" to be the most tiresome words in the
language.

"We do not see that each gyration of Leonard
Bernstein is essential to the most effective conducting," Olin Downes tartly observed, "although it
must be admitted that he very effectively conducts."

Another critic was even more forthright. Watching Bernstein conduct, he said, was like watching

a faithfully exact sound film of a rejuvenated, Ivy League Koussevitzky.

Koussevitzky's conducting was emotional. He pleaded; he exhorted; his baton trembled with excitement; his face and neck became beet-red; when he turned stage left to urge the players to greater exertions, listeners could see the throbbing of the large vein in his forehead.* During the last twenty years of his life, there were listeners at every Koussevitzky concert who fully expected the conductor to drop dead of a coronary before the music was finished.

Reiner's conducting was by contrast as unemotional as anything connected with music could be expected to be. He conducted as if balancing a toothpick on the tip of his baton.

From his two years' study, Bernstein was of course familiar with the impersonal Reiner technique. He had not chosen to imitate it because his impulse, like Koussevitzky's, was to match the gesture to the turn of the musical phrase. In consequence, his conducting was called "choreographic."

Nettled, Bernstein once decided to try Reiner-

---

* A music-loving physician and B. S. O. subscriber once had the interesting experience of giving Koussevitzky a physical examination. The vein, he reported, was merely one which happened to lie near the surface, and its throbbing showed only a normal state of conductorial agitation.

esque economy of means. He beat the time in tight triangles and gave cues with a flip of the hand.

"Routine" was the critical appraisal of the concert, at the conclusion of which several orchestra men inquired anxiously whether he felt all right.

Here Bernstein was brought face to face with the fact that "choreography" which works is to be preferred to Reinerism which doesn't. He resolved the ensuing dilemma by reverting to his old style but averting his face when it was necessary to watch kinescopes of his televised performances.

Another criticism has pursued Bernstein more or less relentlessly ever since: what had a square to do with the world of Broadway and television?

In writing *On the Town,* Bernstein had again stepped out of his frame of reference. Today's conductor is the musical descendant of the baroque *maestro al cembalo,* who guided the performance from a harpsichord and whose word in matters of style and interpretation was law. This Supreme-Court-Justice function lingers on. One who hands down final decisions lends weight to his opinion by being serious, dignified, and authoritative. Not chosen wholly at random were Toscanini's invariable frock coat and striped trousers. In this highly conventionalized world, Bernstein's flirtation with Broadway shocked the piety of the orthodox.

No one was more shocked than Koussevitzky,

although he enjoyed himself hugely at the Boston tryout of *On the Town*. When the final curtain came down, Koussevitzky stopped laughing and took his protégé aside for a blistering three-hour reprimand.

"He was furious with me," Bernstein recalls moodily. Koussevitzky regarded the Broadway theater as frivolous. He berated Bernstein soundly for "wasting" on a musical six months which could have been devoted to his true métier of conducting, or to the writing of a "serious" work.

A six-month stint which resulted in a successful Broadway musical, with all that entailed in the way of financial and other rewards, was not, in Bernstein's opinion, wholly wasted. Nevertheless, such was his respect for Koussevitzky's judgment that when he was offered the conductorship of the New York City Symphony Orchestra, he accepted on the spot.

This orchestra was, in a roundabout way, the consequence of a real-estate foreclosure. The Mecca Temple on West Fifty-fifth Street, a white elephant of an imitation mosque built by a fraternal order during the optimistic twenties, had reverted to the City of New York for back taxes. The sale of so highly specialized and architecturally bizarre a structure appearing to be out of the question, the city sought ways of tapping it for income.

Its assets included a theater seating over 2,000,

with somewhat unpredictable acoustics on account of its tile-and-stucco interior. Leopold Stokowski, always fascinated by acoustical problems, played concerts at the Mecca Temple (renamed Cosmopolitan Opera House) during his season as director of the NBC Symphony Orchestra. He also appeared there with his All-American Youth Orchestra, experimenting tirelessly with acoustical shells and rearranging the instruments for best orchestral effect.

Meanwhile, Lászlo Halász, a Hungarian conductor newly arrived in New York by way of Vienna and St. Louis, convinced music-loving Mayor La Guardia that the building's maze of chapter-rooms could furnish the practice studios, rehearsal stages, costume and scenery storerooms, and offices needed by an opera company.

In 1944, the building became the New York City Center of Music and Drama. Its orchestra played half the week for Stokowski, half for Halász's opera company.

After one season, other interests lured Stokowski away. At the beginning of the 1945-46 season, Bernstein succeeded him and launched a ten-week series of Monday and Tuesday concerts with his "own" orchestra.

For three seasons, Bernstein led the concerts of the New York City Symphony. Although the musicians in the orchestra received union scale, neither

Bernstein nor his soloists were paid a cent. Bernstein appealed, persuasively and successfully, to soloists to donate their services in a worthy cause. It was wonderful while it lasted. Bernstein's programs were lively and wide-ranging. He revived works like Stravinsky's *Oedipus Rex,* which had been out of the New York concert repertoire for years. He programed works by Hindemith, Bartók, Milhaud, Shostakovitch, and Chavez. As a result, an eager, knowledgeable audience gathered at the City Center on Monday and Tuesday evenings.

Such was the impact of Bernstein's New York City Symphony concerts that one critic maintained it would be "a civic calamity if the most adventurous, stimulating and talented conductor to come our way in fifteen years were allowed to be lured to another more attractive post."

In the end it was not a "more attractive post" which ended Bernstein's tenure with the orchestra but a combination of the pressures constantly being exerted upon any symphony orchestra. There was a deficit, of course; and the New York City Symphony had no well-heeled patrons to make it up.

And while the concerts had been an artistic success, Bernstein had been forced to the same sorrowful conclusion as Walter Damrosch with the old New York Symphony and Sir Thomas Beecham with the Brooklyn Philharmonic: that, for New

York City, one resident orchestra was plenty. If talent and unsparing energy could have made a go of the New York City Symphony concerts, Bernstein would have succeeded. But not even talent can contend with the forces of musical economics. In the spring of 1948, Bernstein decided to call it quits.

His letter of resignation created a furore. Wounded civic pride asked how such things could be. Newspapers again raised the old question of why the nation's largest and richest city could not support a second symphony orchestra. If Philadelphia, for example, was able to maintain one orchestra, New York on a per capita basis ought to have three.

Bernstein was urged to withdraw his resignation while a solution was sought. Heads of the City Center pondered, then came up with a compromise plan whereby the concerts would continue, but with a reduced group of chamber orchestra size.

Quite sensibly, Bernstein refused to have anything to do with this arrangement. The New York City Symphony operation, he pointed out, was skimpy enough as it was. By taking jobs with the orchestra, players were guaranteed only ten weeks' work and were obliged to free-lance precariously for the rest of the season. Expansion, not contraction, of the New York City Symphony was the need.

Everyone agreed in principle; but no way could be found of footing the bill, and the New York City Symphony concerts became history.

The three years with the orchestra, however, had given Bernstein a valuable postgraduate course in the psychology of orchestral musicians. And conducting, Rodzinski maintained, is seventy-five per cent applied psychology.

When Bernstein became conductor of the New York City Symphony, he was twenty-seven. Youth is, for a conductor, a not unmixed blessing. Fernando Previtali, equally successful as conductor and teacher of conducting at Rome's Sta. Cecilia Academy, holds that the commonest fault of young conductors is that they talk too much, or rather, that they say the wrong things. "As a young conductor, you can make any point you like, if you do it in strictly musical terms," Previtali once said. "*Più forte, meno mosso,* and so forth. But if you undertake to tell an orchestra of players twice your age what the music 'means,' you are"—Previtali executed the pantomime of drawing a revolver from his hip pocket—"dead."

On this point, Bernstein concurs: "I think this is true of any conductor, of whatever age."

Equally vexing was the problem of discipline, without which an orchestra falls apart. Toscanini solved it by erupting in a Vesuvius of abusive epithets, of which "shoemakers" and "assassins" were mild examples. The men would take it from Toscanini; he was a living link with the Great Tradition. He had played 'cello when Verdi led the orchestra at La Scala; Puccini had selected him to lead premières of his operas. But what held for Toscanini did not necessarily hold for every young Harvard *cum laude.*

Bernstein was shrewd enough to see the problem clearly, and resourceful enough to cope with it.

He strove not to put himself on a pedestal as The Maestro, but to imbue the players with his own enthusiasm. In the back of his mind may have been the recollection of Mitropoulos taking the Boston Symphony Orchestra into his confidence, and the eye-opening discovery that there were other ways of leading a rehearsal than Koussevitzkian tantrums.

"Lenny was one of the boys," says a musician who played in the New York City Symphony. "He was never the maestro. Nobody ever called him anything but Lenny. He treated the musicians absolutely as equals. And he was generally liked and respected."

Another factor in Bernstein's favor was a ready mother-wit which served and still serves him well.

When a nervous soprano found heavy going the long, sustained phrases of the "Et incarnatus est" from Mozart's C Minor Mass, Bernstein stopped the orchestra to ask solicitously:

"First timesies?"

That broke up the soprano, but it also broke the ice, and when order could be restored, "Et incarnatus est" proceeded without a hitch.

A musician worn out with doubling between concerts and midnight recording sessions dropped off to sleep during a concert, just before a brief but important solo.

He awoke with a start and asked a neighbor: "Freddie, where are we?"

"Letter H," Freddie replied.

This was a disaster. His solo had come shortly after Letter G in the score.

The musician expected, knew he deserved, and would have accepted meekly, a ferocious bawling-out from Bernstein. But Bernstein said not a word.

At the repeat performance, however, when the musician played his solo brilliantly, Bernstein opened his eyes very wide and spread his left hand in a gesture which said as plainly as words: "Where were you last time?"

For a time thereafter, when members of the orchestra met, they greeted each other with the where-were-you-last-time gesture.

And the offending player made it a point not to fall asleep when Bernstein was conducting.

There can be times when, for no apparent reason, the whole orchestra appears to be dragging its feet. One man may have family troubles, another has a note coming due at the bank, someone else's feet hurt, and so on. Their sour mood infects everyone else, and the rehearsal never gets off the ground.

On one such occasion, Bernstein was seeking in vain the light-fingered, delicate grace needed for Mendelssohn's "Midsummer Night's Dream" music. The orchestra's playing remained sulky and heavy-handed. The Puckish touch was missing.

"What this orchestra needs," Bernstein observed, "is more fairies."

When the laughter had subsided, the players went to work in earnest and gave Bernstein the effect he wanted.

The New York City Symphony concerts, in addition to their value for Bernstein as conducting experience, had another lasting result. A young lady from Chile, who had come to New York to study piano, was told by a friend: "There is someone you ought to marry. His name is Leonard Bernstein."

"Fantastic," the young lady said. But she agreed to hear Bernstein perform at the City Center.

Chapter 8

BERNSTEIN at this point was whirling about the globe like a dominant seventh chord in orbit. Conducting the New York City Symphony did not by any means drain his creative energy; it was merely a central base of operations around which his other activities revolved.

His guest appearance in Pittsburgh, to conduct his "Jeremiah" Symphony, was followed by re-engagement for a seven-week series the following season. He appeared with the orchestras of Los Angeles, St. Louis, Rochester, Philadelphia, and Boston. He was a regular guest conductor of the New York Philharmonic, and a fixture at Tanglewood, where he had been Koussevitzky's assistant since 1946, during the summer.

One continent was in fact not large enough to

contain him. When postwar travel restrictions eased, he won an ovation with the Staatsoper Orchestra in Munich; led a concert of U.S. music at the 1947 Brussels Film Festival; appeared with the London Philharmonic; and, before the Iron Curtain closed on that part of the world, led the Czech Philharmonic Orchestra at the Prague Festivals of 1946 and 1947.

"That concert in Munich must have been the most remarkable of all," an eyewitness recalled years later. "Bernstein had been invited to conduct there by Georg Solti, who was then head of the Bavarian State Opera. You have to remember the state of affairs in Germany just after the war. The orchestra was on a hunger strike. Two players had fainted at rehearsal the day before Bernstein arrived. Bernstein had two strikes against him, for being American and Jewish. But once he'd rehearsed the orchestra, they were enthusiastic and ready to go.

"They also played one concert, with a pitiful Dachau band of seventeen people, at a Displaced Persons camp near Munich. The hall was packed beyond belief. Bernstein played on a terrible upright piano, out of tune, with half the keys missing. He made it sound great. The applause was tremendous; they nearly tore the place apart.

"And, remember, when Bernstein led the Staatsoper Orchestra he wasn't the world-famous conductor of the New York Philharmonic, just a youngster on the way up. By sheer magnetism and force of personality he pulled a good performance out of a hostile orchestra in very discouraging surroundings. I think of that whenever I hear somebody call Bernstein's career a fluke."

Bernstein won the admiration of Dutch listeners by his resourcefulness when a French railway strike prevented his soloist, violinist Nathan Milstein, from making a scheduled appearance at Scheveningen. Bernstein quickly substituted the Ravel Piano Concerto, conducting from the keyboard. For good measure, he played his Suite from *On the Town*.

At this stage of his career, Bernstein was beginning to find himself overwhelmed by the sheer mass of detail calling for immediate attention. A busy and successful conductor is one of the few beings on the planet who can tell you with reasonable certainty where he will be and what he will be doing twelve or eighteen months from now. But by the same token, dovetailing timetables with concerts, arranging hotel reservations, booking plane, train, and steamship passages, keeping track of scores, evening clothes and so forth can become almost a full time occupation in itself. There was fan mail to be answered, and business appointments needed looking after. Bernstein found he could not cope with it all.

In his student days, it had been second nature for Bernstein, in moments of perplexity, to lay his problems before Helen Coates. He now sounded out his teacher and confidante. Would she be willing to leave Boston and come to New York as his secretary?

Miss Coates would, and did, and does, in a manner to refute the notion that musicians are fuzzy-minded folk incapable of coping with practical problems.

To describe Miss Coates's attitude toward her former pupil as "doting" seems an overstatement. She views her brilliant employer with calm acceptance. No one, apparently, has been less astonished by Bernstein's rise to world-wide fame than Helen Coates.

During the four years 1945-48, Bernstein's creative output was small. A glance at his touring itinerary makes it easy to understand why.

He did, however, find time to compose another score for Ballet Theater, with choreography by Jerome Robbins. The new ballet, *Facsimile*, had its first performance at the Broadway Theater on October 24, 1946.

It is possible that Bernstein was somewhat staggered by the scenario which his collaborator laid before him. A complete about-face from the high-spirited doings of *Fancy Free*, it was a wry sermon on a text out of Ramon y Cajal: "Small inward treasure does he possess who, to feel alive, needs every hour the tumult of the street, the emotion of the theater and the small talk of society."

The cast was to consist of only three dancers, a woman and two men. As the scene opened, the woman was on a deserted beach, bored to distraction with herself and her surroundings. When the first man turned up, she was bored with him, too, until the second appeared as his rival. Their quarrel worked up to a fight, until the woman—whom there was no pleasing, it seemed—wearied of the combat, called it to a halt, and sent her frustrated suitors about their business. As the scene ended, she was as bored as when it began.

This epic of ennui was not the sort of thing calculated to fire one's imagination. And it would have been difficult for anyone so thoroughly alive as Bernstein to write the bored-sounding music which the scenario seemed to demand.

Nevertheless, the score which Bernstein turned out was probing, thoughtful, and not quite like anything he had written before. Bernstein is no longer the sprightly, entertaining man of the theater; he is very much the serious composer, writing earnestly in contemporary idiom.

Although *Facsimile,* because of its style and content, inevitably did not have the wide appeal of *Fancy Free,* it is a score of considerable interest and a milestone in the evolution of Bernstein's creative personality.

"Haskivenu," for four-part mixed voices, cantor, and organ, was one of a series of liturgical works commissioned annually by the Park Avenue Synagogue. It had its first performance there May 11, 1945. Besides showing Bernstein's awareness of his Jewish heritage, and his readiness to draw upon its cultural richness, the score disclosed yet another side of Bernstein's expanding talent. The earnest symphonist and amusing Broadway showman could write music of power and dignity, appropriate for the Temple service.

A set of pieces written during 1947-48 suggest a borrowing, conscious or unconscious, from Hindemith. There is no exact English equivalent for *Gebrauchsmusik*, the name Hindemith applied to music written for a specific purpose, such as teaching, or because the literature for a given instrument or combination of instruments happens to be scant. An approximation would be "purposeful" or "functional music."

Bernstein's *Gebrauchsmusik* took the form of "Elegy for Mippy I" for horn and piano; "Elegy for Mippy II" for solo trombone; "Fanfare for Bima" for trumpet, horn, trombone, and tuba; "Rondo for Lifey" for trumpet and piano; and "Waltz for Mippy III" for tuba and piano.

All the dedications are to dogs. Mippy I, II, and III belonged to his brother, Burton; Lifey to Judy Holliday; Bima to the Koussevitzkys.

If their titles are dogs, the pieces themselves

are not. The repertoire for brass instruments is so limited, and the pieces are written with such expert knowledge of the instruments and their resources, that they fill a definite need. G. Schirmer, Inc., Bernstein's publishers, beam happily when the brass pieces are mentioned.

"La Bonne Cuisine," a cycle of four songs, had its first performance on October 1, 1948, at the New York recital of soprano Marion Bell. The cycle actually is a setting of four recipes from a French cookbook which Bernstein found in a house he had rented one summer at Tanglewood. The French can be eloquent when writing about food, and Bernstein was so charmed by the work's literary style that he began setting it to music. A tasty and amusing concoction, "La Bonne Cuisine" is not a work of major importance, and probably was not intended to be.

Four more "anniversaries" for piano completed Bernstein's 1945-48 output. The new works were dedicated to Johnny Mehegan, David Diamond, Helen Coates, and Felicia Montealegre, of whom more was to be heard very soon.

In 1948, Bernstein set to work on a big new work, his second symphony. The inspiration for it came from W. H. Auden's "baroque eclogue," titled *The Age of Anxiety*.

Bernstein had read the Auden poem, and from that moment the composing of a symphony on the same theme assumed, in his words, "an almost compulsive quality." Although he was constantly in motion, he kept working at his *Age of Anxiety* score. Parts of it were written in Taos, Philadelphia, Richmond, and Tel Aviv. Finishing touches were added during a tour with the Pittsburgh Symphony, and on the last page of the score Bernstein wrote: "NYC—the first day of spring!"

The first performance took place in Boston on April 8, 1949, with Serge Koussevitzky, to whom the work is dedicated, leading the Boston Symphony Orchestra, and with Bernstein as piano soloist.

Bernstein explained that his symphony was, like Auden's poem, "a record of our difficult and problematical search for faith." Its first section, "The Seven Ages," introduces four characters, three men and a girl, who meet in a New York bar. It is in the form of an introduction and fourteen variations. In Variations One through Seven, the state of man is discussed from the viewpoint of each of the four characters. The remainder of the variations represent a symbolic quest for certainty.

In the next section, "The Dirge," all four are in a taxi, bound for the girl's apartment to have a nightcap. Here they lament the loss of "Big Dad," the father-image leader who knew all the answers. In "The Masque," after trying vainly to shake off their feelings of guilt and weariness, the characters disperse. In the final section, "Epilogue," each resolves his doubts and uncertainties in one way or another.

The Age of Anxiety was the most complex and in many ways most interesting score which Bernstein had yet written. The music has enormous variety. Jazz rubs elbows with Schoenbergian dissonance and almost Brahmsian romanticism. These disparate elements are united and unified by the composer with sure-handed craftsmanship.

Whether or not the work should be called a symphony is perhaps a hair-splitting quibble. That it is excellent music for the theater was shown by the ease with which Jerome Robbins fashioned an effective ballet to be danced to the *Age of Anxiety* music. Again, Bernstein's musical instinct seemed to be impelling him toward the theater, although four or five years were still to elapse before the notion at the back of his mind was clarified and set down in writing—that the writing of symphonies is, at this particular time and place in musical history at least, a mug's game. ("Imaginary Conversations" No. 2, "Whatever Happened to that Great American Symphony?")

Auden, by the way, contrary to a widespread impression was not "L. P." of the Imaginary Conversations," the lyric poet whom Bernstein frustrates at every turn by giving the best lines to himself.

116

Auden speaks with respect of "Mr. Bairnsteen," whose music he has heard with great interest. It seems clear, however, that he does not feel Bernstein's *Age of Anxiety* has superseded his own.

Chapter 9

𝒜MONG HIS MANY conducting engagements, one concert of special significance for Bernstein took place May 1, 1947. This was his debut with the Palestine Symphony Orchestra in Jerusalem.

It was also the first performance there of Bernstein's "Jeremiah" Symphony. The performance was nearly canceled because the score had been lost in transit. Another copy, however, was hastily flown from New York in time to save the day.

Eyewitnesses at the concert described the ovation received by Bernstein as second only to that accorded Toscanini.

To understand fully what this meant in terms of a Jerusalem audience, it should be recalled that Toscanini, after his famous refusal to conduct at Bayreuth after the Hitler government came to power in Germany, had devoted much time and care to the new, struggling Palestine Symphony, founded by Bronislaw Hubermann in 1936 around a nucleus of refugee musicians from central Europe. Toscanini had conducted the orchestra without fee, had scrounged music and instruments from America and Italy, and in various ways had lent it the prestige of his world-famous name. He is in consequence the musical idol of Palestine. To receive a Toscanini-like ovation meant one had conquered Jerusalem.

And Bernstein had. New York *Times* correspondent Clifton Daniel cabled that audiences were "sentimentally captivated by his qualities of being young, handsome, talented and Jewish."

Bernstein in fact stood with his people at a tremendous turning point in history. Only by a strong effort of imagination and consideration of the historical background can a non-Jew hope to form an idea of what Bernstein's presence meant.

The destruction of Solomon's Temple by the Romans in 70 A.D., following the furious Maccabean wars, ushered in the period which Jews call the *diaspora,* or dispersion. Scattered abroad, Jews remembered Jerusalem. It may be true, as Vincent Sheean has commented, that nostalgia for Jerusalem was accompanied by the desire to live somewhere else. But the nostalgia was always there. The Passover service ends with the words, "L'shona Habaa b'Yrushalayim," meaning, "Next year we shall celebrate the Passover in Jerusalem." Now the energetic and tenacious folk who had made this pledge through many hundreds of years were seeing it actually come about.

Bernstein was a part of this—and something more. He represented help and encouragement from abroad. This was of special importance when it became clear that the British forces which had maintained precarious peace in the Holy Land would be withdrawn when the British mandate expired, leaving Jews and Arabs to shoot it out.

In those tense days, it was not to be wondered at that Bernstein's presence should have a powerful impact on audiences. Shirley, who accompanied him, remembers well the highly charged atmosphere of the times.

"It was so emotional," she recalls. "Lenny and I cried for three weeks."

Today, to describe a really spectacular triumph, Bernstein will say simply: "It was like Israel."

When Bernstein returned in September, 1948, the new state of Israel was in being, and in battle. The Palestine Symphony had been reconstituted the Israel Philharmonic Orchestra, partly with the aid of friends in America. Among its original sponsors were two New York music critics, the late Robert C. Bagar and the present writer.*

* Facts should be kept in perspective. Sponsorship of the first season cost fifteen dollars. The next year it became one hundred

With the renamed orchestra, Bernstein toured
Israel, playing and conducting not only in Tel
Aviv, Jerusalem, and other cities but in situations
dangerously close to the firing line.

If Israel had cheered Bernstein before, it now
embraced him as a national hero. His sheer raw
courage in performing under difficult and dangerous conditions is still remembered with admiration.

Bernstein and the orchestra were at times only
forty-eight hours behind advancing troops. Bodies
of dead Arabs lined the road when they went to
Beersheba.

During the fighting in the Negev, Bernstein de-
termined to play a concert for troops there. Because
of the hazardous nature of the assignment, he
called for volunteers. Thirty players responded,
piled their instruments in an armored bus, and set
out for the fighting zone.

The story was told of this event that word of
the impending concert got around so quickly
among music-hungry troops that Egyptian spotter
planes radioed word to their headquarters that the
Israeli army was massing for a new attack.

Helen Coates, who was with Bernstein on the
tour of Israel, remembers a dramatic scene in Beer-

fifty, immediately pricing newspapermen out of the market. At a
sponsors' roll call, impresario Sol Hurok eased a sticky moment
for a newspaperman-sponsor by going to the rostrum and mur-
muring, "Press."

sheba—Bernstein, surrounded by 5,000 soldiers in an amphitheater formed by archaeological excavations, playing Gershwin's "Rhapsody in Blue" just at sunset.

At the end of a concert in Jerusalem, the garrison commander pinned the Jerusalem insignia on his lapel, while 2,000 men and women in uniform cheered for half an hour.

During a concert in Rehovot, there were two air raid alarms. Bernstein, who was conducting a Beethoven piano concerto from the keyboard, never missed a beat. (Neither did the audience, Bernstein recalls, which included Dr. Chaim Weizmann, President of Israel.)

Bernstein's performance under fire can best be appreciated by those who have dabbled in public performance enough to know what even mild stage fright does to one's nerves and fingers.

When complimented on the performance, Bernstein parried the compliment with a jest.

"I never played such an adagio," he said. "I thought it was my swan song."

But it was not, and the energetic young conductor-pianist kept on the move. When he was not touring with the Israel Philharmonic, he spent his free evenings entertaining in hospitals and military camps. Far from wilting under the pressure, Bernstein flourished. According to Peter Gradenwitz of the *Times,* Bernstein "seems to be having the time of his life."

The front line performances were exciting; but something else made an even profounder impression on Bernstein. It was meeting a Jew who could, as Bernstein put it, "afford the luxury of being illiterate."

In all countries of the world, Bernstein pointed out, there was never a question whether Jewish children should be educated. Their wits needed to be sharp as a matter of survival. Now, at home in Israel, a man could live the life of a farmer, moving to the slow-changing rhythms of the seasons, and not greatly caring about anything else.

"He was a *paisano*, a man of the soil," Bernstein says. "It was wonderful."

When his tour with the orchestra ended late in 1948, Bernstein found himself a national hero in Israel.

His close and friendly relationship with the Israel Philharmonic has continued. In the summer of 1950, he made a seven-week guest appearance. In December of that year, when the orchestra arrived for its first U.S. tour, its conductors were Koussevitzky and Bernstein. The tour, which began in Washington on January 7, 1951, took the Israel Philharmonic on a brilliantly successful tour of some forty U.S. cities.

Bernstein also conducted the orchestra during its return engagement, and has returned to Israel at various times for concerts there.

In 1948, however, his dangerous tour of duty

with the orchestra was merely one event, however striking, in a season crammed full of activity. From Israel, he was to fly to Pittsburgh, where he was to make a seven-week guest appearance with the orchestra. Then back to New York to lead the NBC Symphony Orchestra, with Jascha Heifetz as soloist, at a testimonial dinner at the Waldorf-Astoria honoring Dr. Chaim Weizmann. And another Waldorf concert, this one by the Tanglewood Alumni String Orchestra, to honor Koussevitzky.

Meanwhile—there are phases of Bernstein's career in which so much is going on as to make orderly narrative all but impossible—early in 1949 there came the first official announcement that Bernstein was at work on a big new project. It was to be a musical based on Shakespeare's *Romeo and Juliet,* with the Montagues and Capulets changed to feuding rowdies on Manhattan's Lower East Side.

In the summer, Bernstein was again at Tanglewood, carrying a full schedule of conducting, and discussing with Koussevitzky a project close to the older conductor's heart.

Koussevitzky had all his life been a champion and popularizer of contemporary works. As a young man in pre-revolutionary Russia, he had with the aid of his first wife's considerable fortune founded a publishing house and organized his own symphony orchestra. In a chartered steamer, he toured up and down the Volga, sometimes performing in towns where no concert had ever been heard before. In Paris, following the revolution, he had founded another orchestra and a publishing house specializing in contemporary works. As musical director of the Boston Symphony Orchestra, he had tirelessly brought out new works, often avant-garde pieces which made directors and orchestra subscribers very unhappy.

Now Koussevitzky was planning to ensure that aid to new music would continue beyond his own lifetime. The Koussevitzky Foundation planned to make an initial gift of $100,000 to the Library of Congress to encourage musical composition. Would Bernstein serve on the board of directors?

Bernstein said he would be delighted.

The end of the Tanglewood summer season is a good time and a pleasant place in which to collect one's thoughts. And Bernstein in the summer of 1949 had a good deal to think about.

His career as a conductor, limited in its early stages by wartime conditions to the United States, had branched out to make him a "name" conductor of international reputation. As a composer, he had to his credit two prize-winning symphonies (*The Age of Anxiety* had won the 1948-49 Hornblit Prize of $1,000 for the best new work played by the B. S. O. during the season), a hit musical, and two successfully performed ballet scores, not to mention the works in smaller forms. And he had established himself as a pianist of outstanding promise.

Nevertheless, Bernstein at this time was depressed and unhappy. His experience with the New York City Symphony still rankled. He had put an enormous amount of time, work, and worry into the orchestra. Its failure, although due to factors beyond his control, remained a disappointment.

Worst of all was his obsessive sense that time was running out. On August 25, 1949, he would be thirty-one years old; and he felt that he had not amounted to very much.

Chapter 10

*I*T IS HARD TO SAY with precision, after the lapse
of years, just when Bernstein discovered that he
was an expounder as well as a maker of music,
with a special flair for capturing the interest of
young audiences.

Certainly this flair was much in evidence on an
October afternoon in 1946 when Bernstein led the
senior orchestra of New York's High School of
Music and Art in a rehearsal of the "Leonore"
Overture No. 3.

Bernstein walked into the rehearsal hall with a
breezy hello, removed his jacket, and asked the
youthful players to stop him "if I make any
mistakes."

The rehearsal went swimmingly. At one point
Bernstein stopped the orchestra.

"You're hastening your crescendoes," said the

twenty-seven-year-old maestro. "That is one of the sins of youth."

The students loved it. At the rehearsal's conclusion, they gave Bernstein an ovation. "It's wonderful—that's all I can say," one student musician observed.

As Bernstein's sphere of activity widened, it was natural that it should include the newly developing field of television. In addition to his musical gifts, Bernstein made a good impression under the merciless scrutiny of the TV cameras. Not everyone does. When one famous orchestra and its equally famous conductor made their television debuts, a nationwide audience discovered that it was the conductor's habit to chew jujubes in time to the music.

Bernstein, on the other hand, proved photogenic, with something of the actor's quality. His lean, mobile features are capable of so wide a range of expression that, leafing through a file of Bernstein photographs, one can hardly believe them to be all of the same man.

Like an actor, Bernstein is on the stage even when he is off. So simple a gesture as lighting a cigarette is done with an unconscious eye to pictorial effect. He assumes graceful postures with the easy, unconscious posing that comes from many years of public appearance.

Bernstein is made acutely unhappy when this

fact is pointed out, but he is deluding only himself if he thinks he is the mousy-professor type. No one who has made as many stage appearances as Bernstein can remain unchanged; the stage leaves its mark no less than the parade ground. And it is not pose or affectation, but merely the reaction of a man who knows he is on display, is used to the sensation, and does not mind.

Bernstein's speech, too, is somewhat theatrical, a curious but interesting combination of broad-A Bostonian and the racy slang of show business.

This combining of apparent incongruities in fact crops up in many areas, as a result of Bernstein's inquisitive, wide-ranging intelligence and his solid classical education at Boston Latin School and Harvard. He shares the knack of the Canadian humorist Stephen Leacock for making a point through odd, unexpected juxtapositions.

By describing an imaginary conversation between the Keeper of the Royal Swans and the Keeper of the Privy Seal, Leacock could give in a few words an impression of venerable British institutions more vivid than a lengthy essay.

In rather similar fashion, Bernstein later in his career to describe blues form on an *Omnibus* telecast would improvise the "Macbeth Blues":

> I will not be afraid of death and bane,
> I said I will not be afraid of death and bane,
> Till Birnam Forest come to Dunsinane.

129

But that would come later, when Bernstein had acquired the finesse and the sure hand of expert musical showmanship. In the early stages, he was still finding his way about the new medium—as, indeed, everyone else in television was—getting to know orchestras and audiences better, and occasionally wincing at comments like Virgil Thomson's description of him as a "musical Dick Tracy."

Bernstein had demonstrated, however—and Thomson had conceded—that he possessed the all-important conductor's attribute of a good ear.

Bernstein does not have absolute pitch, that curious and inexplicable gift which enables some people to identify any note or combination of notes they hear, or to sound any note requested. It is a gift which no amount of study can acquire. Those who have it have no idea how it is done; they only know they have been able to do it ever since they learned the notes of the scale. It seems to have no direct relation to musicality. Many great musicians (Wagner, for example) have been without it, and some possess it whose talents are slight.

What Bernstein does have is a sense of relative pitch so keen as to be almost as reliable as the absolute pitch which he lacks. It is as if, having once heard the oboe's A-440, he can retain it in his ear for the rest of the day. His phenomenal abilities in this regard perplex musicians whenever the subject of Bernstein and absolute pitch comes up. Does he or doesn't he? Although she had worked with him at the piano since his teens, Helen Coates had to ask him to be sure.

"I'm not sure if he has it," says another musician who has worked closely with Bernstein, and who himself possesses absolute pitch. "All I can say is, he's got a terrific ear on him."

Bernstein also demonstrated early in his career an unusual sense of tempo, in which conductors vary widely. How widely, indeed, was first appreciated in the early days of radio, when the networks were beginning to broadcast symphonic music. As an aid in program planning, it occurred to somebody to time the major symphonic works in performance.

To the broadcasters' astonishment, the stopwatch revealed that two conductors, or even the same conductor, hardly ever did a work at exactly the same speed twice running. Variations of mood and state of mind showed in the conductor's beat. Few could match the late Artur Bodanzky, who used to win bets at the Metropolitan by bringing the second act of *Die Walküre* to a close in one hour, no more, no less.

Toscanini's sense of tempo was sometimes erratic. Once the pace was set, he would maintain it through thick and thin; but the tempo itself could vary.

This fact puzzled Bernstein, who had observed

that during a Toscanini broadcast of the "Love Scene" from Berlioz's *Romeo and Juliet,* the tempo was much slower than in Toscanini's Victor recording of the same work. (Though he hardly ever listens to records today, aside from playbacks of his own recording sessions, Bernstein studied records attentively in his early years.)

Since he had met Toscanini, Bernstein asked permission to call to discuss tempo and other problems of *Romeo and Juliet,* which he was planning to conduct at one of his own concerts.

The older conductor sent back a cordial invitation to come to the Villa Pauline, his house in Riverdale overlooking a wide sweep of the Hudson River. Here Bernstein spent a fascinating October afternoon in 1949 with Toscanini.

"He was in rare form," Bernstein recalls, "running up the stairs two at a time and bouncing all over the place." Bernstein, wheezing with asthma, was hard put to keep up.

One can picture the two of them, the dark-haired, intense young American and the white-haired Italian, speaking quaint English in a voice hoarse from years of shouting at orchestras, polishing his pince-nez and beaming paternally as Bernstein laid his problem before him.

There were so many anomalies in the *Romeo and Juliet* score as to lead Bernstein to suspect he had gotten hold of a carelessly edited version. At one point, for example, there was an instruction

At 4, his musical talent yet to be discovered, it was already clear that Leonard was a very bright boy. (Courtesy of Samuel J. Bernstein)

Bernstein, age 11, and his father on vacation. The boy had just found his spectacular affinity for music. (Courtesy of Samuel J. Bernstein)

A family group shows, left to right, Burton Bernstein, Mr. and Mrs. Samuel J. Bernstein, and Leonard. (Courtesy of Samuel J. Bernstein)

A midwinter vacation, with 11-year-old Leonard on the fence. His father wanted him to go into business (Courtesy of Samuel J Bernstein)

Bernstein at 16, already finding his musical talent an asset at the celebrated Boston Latin School. (Courtesy of Samuel J. Bernstein)

A close-up of Bernstein at the piano. The same subject has fascinated hundreds of photographers since then. (Courtesy of Samuel J. Bernstein)

Young Harvardian meets B.S.O. conductor. Friendship with
Koussevitzky would help to mold Bernstein's career.
(Courtesy of Samuel J. Bernstein)

Bernstein at Jennie Tourel's 1943 Town Hall recital, unaware he would lead the Philharmonic next day. (Photo by Larry Gordon Studios)

Concertmaster John Corigliano and other Philharmonic players
compliment Bernstein after his brilliant 1943 debut.
(Photo by the New York Times)

By 1945, autographing photos was no novelty for Bernstein, but this
one was special: "For Mother, Xmas, 1945."
(Courtesy of Samuel J. Bernstein)

Bernstein and W. H. Auden in 1949 discussing *The Age of Anxiety*, written by Auden, composed by Bernstein. (Photo by Ben Greenhaus)

Members of a 1952 cast of *Trouble in Tahiti* rehearse the opera under the composer's knowledgeable direction. (Photo by the New York Times)

When Bernstein led *Medea,* with Maria Callas, at La Scala in 1953, skeptics foresaw disaster. They were wrong. (Photo by Erio Piccagliani)

Clarinetist Benny Goodman was soloist with Bernstein at a Symphony of the Air Concert in Carnegie Hall in 1955. (Photo by the New York Times)

The combination of Bernstein and Louis Armstrong packed Lewisohn Stadium for a concert in August, 1956. (Photo by Columbia Records)

By 1956, the undergraduate whom Dimitri Mitropoulos called "genius boy" was a colleague. (Photo by Henry Rapisarda, Impact Photos, Inc.)

Bernstein had recorded even before his Philharmonic debut. By January, 1958, he was an old hand in record studios.
(Photo by Columbia Records)

Bernstein with Lillian Hellman and Tyrone Guthrie at a 1956
Candide rehearsal. (Photo by Friedman-Abeles)

But *West Side Story* made
up for *Candide*. Jerome
Robbins, Harold Prince,
Chita Rivera, Bernstein.
(Courtesy Griffith & Prince
Productions)

L-R: Lyricist Sondheim, writer Laurents, producers Griffith and Prince, Bernstein, and Robbins at *WSS* rehearsal.
(Photo by Friedman-Abeles)

The starting point: Bernstein's manuscript for the dance-hall sequence, a powerful section of *West Side Story*. (Courtesy of Leonard Bernstein)

A revival of *West Side Story*, Bernstein conducting, was one of the hits of the 1959-60 season. (Courtesy Griffith & Prince Productions)

The Bernsteins at home, December, 1956. (Whitestone Photo)

Fascinated by folk music, Bernstein "sat in" with natives at La Paz, Bolivia, during 1958 Philharmonic tour. (Photo by Columbia Records)

After the 1958 Philharmonic concert in Santiago, Chile, Bernstein needed help to fend off admirers. (Photo courtesy of the New York Philharmonic)

Dr. Manuel Prado, President of Peru, congratulated Bernstein after his
1958 Lima performance as conductor-pianist.
(Photo by Columbia Records)

A 1958 studio performance shows the evident joy in music-making which endeared Bernstein to nationwide TV viewers.
(Photo by Columbia Records)

Isaac Stern was soloist when Bernstein's *Serenade* was introduced in 1959 to listeners in this country and abroad. (Photo by Columbia Records)

Two American world figures in music, Bernstein and pianist Van Cliburn, highlighted the 1958-59 New York Philharmonic season. (Photo by Bert Bial)

"The Ruins of Athens" inspir
Byron and Beethoven. Bernste
sensed their magic during 19
Philharmonic tour. (Photo
Columbia Records)

Three American conductor-pianists, Thomas Schippers, Bernstein, and
Seymour Lipkin, with the Philharmonic in Athens.
(Photo by Columbia Records)

The American continent could not contain Bernstein's TV shows. One was filmed in the Teatro La Fenice, Venice, 1959.
(Photo by Columbia Records)

A reception committee with flowers greeted the Bernsteins at Warsaw airport during the Philharmonic's 1959 tour.
(Photo by Zb. Lewandowski)

Violinist Tossy Spivakovsky, Bernstein, and composer Roger Sessions discussing Sessions' just-rehearsed violin concerto.
(Photo by Bert Bial)

Bernstein at Brandeis University, 1952. (Photo courtesy of
Brandeis University)

Bernstein and pianist Seymour Lipkin take a bow in the Great Hall of
Moscow's Tchaikovsky Conservatory, 1959.
(Photo by Columbia Records)

Bernstein embraced by the composer after his performance of
Shostakovitch's 5th Symphony, Moscow, September, 1959.
(Photo by Columbia Records)

The meeting with Boris Pasternak; at right is Mrs. Bernstein.
(Photo by Columbia Records)

Just back from the Philharmonic's tour behind the Iron Curtain,
there was no rest. In October he was at it again.
(Photo by Columbia Records)

Chilly weather sometimes forced Bernstein to exchange his favored polo shirt for a leather jacket. (Photo by Irv Haberman, the CBS Television Network)

In December, 1959, Bernstein joined manager-pianist Carlos Moseley, to listen as businessman-pianist David M. Keiser played Bach. (Photo by the New York Times)

Paul Desmond, alto sax, Bernstein, and Dave Brubeck recording
Howard Brubeck's *Dialogues for Jazz Combo and Orchestra*.
(Photo by Columbia Records)

With Robert Merrill as baritone soloist, Bernstein and the
Philharmonic record Bloch's *Sacred Service*, April, 1960.
(Photo by Columbia Records)

Glenn Gould was piano soloist with Bernstein and the Philharmonic at a recording session in May, 1959. (Photo by Columbia Records)

On the Town hands Nancy Walker, Bernstein, Adolph Green, and Betty Comden were on hand to record it in May, 1960.
(Photo by Columbia Records)

On his way back from Moscow, Bernstein met Dr. Robert Oppenheimer and George Kennan backstage in Basel, Switzerland. (Photo by Columbia Records)

Bruno Walter and Bernstein chat in April, 1960, seventeen years after Bernstein first filled in for Walter. (Photo by Columbia Records)

Bernstein was greeted in grand style by four Hawaiian girls during the Philharmonic's tour of the islands. (Photo by Jerry Y. Chong/Camera Hawaii)

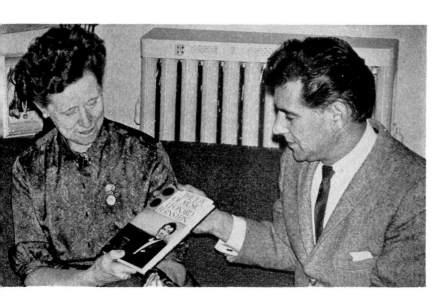

Helen Coates, to whom the book is dedicated, receives a copy of *The Joy of Music* from author Bernstein. (Photo by George Cserna.)

Bernstein and his wife make a glamorous couple in formal dress at the opening night of the Metropolitan Opera.
(Photo by the New York Times)

for the violins to remove their mutes, but no indication of how the mutes got there in the first place.

Toscanini, whose phenomenal memory was a legend in the musical world, from his vast storehouse of knowledge produced helpful answers to most of the questions. But when Bernstein summoned up courage to ask about the tempo, Toscanini was genuinely perplexed. Clearly there was only one possible speed at which to play the "Love Scene"—the correct, or Toscanini, tempo.

However, he promised to compare the transcription of his broadcast with the Victor recording.

Bernstein treasures the letter which he received a few days later, written in red ink in Toscanini's unmistakable bold handwriting:

October 13, 1949

My dear Bernstein:

I compared the Victor recording of the Love Scene from Berlioz' "Romeo and Juliet" with the broadcast and confirmed the fact that the Victor is much faster.

And I confirmed another fact—namely—that every man, no matter the importance of his intelligence, can be from time to time a little stupid . . . So is the case of the old Toscanini.

Your kind visit and dear letter made me very, very happy . . . I felt myself 40 years younger.

I hope to see you very soon, and it will give me a great amount of pleasure. Most cordially, believe me, dear Bernstein, yours ever,

A. Toscanini

133

Those who relished Bernstein's account of this incident were reminded of a story which NBC Symphony players brought back from their South American tour with Toscanini.

To pass the time at sea, a group of players invited the Maestro to hear a short-wave broadcast from London. An orchestra was halfway through the "Eroica" Symphony. The Maestro's face darkened as he listened. What *porco* of a conductor could be taking the music at that insane speed? When the performance ended, he was livid with fury and ready to smash the radio.

Then a bland British voice announced: "You have just heard a recording by the BBC Symphony Orchestra, conducted by Arturo Toscanini."

Chapter 11

ONE OF THE CLICHÉS of stage, films, radio, and television is that in which it is obvious to everybody that a boy and girl are meant for each other —except to the boy and girl themselves.

In Bernstein's case, as might have been expected, this rather trite situation received a fresh twist. It was clearly apparent to the girl.

They met at a post-concert party in Douglaston, Long Island. Claudio Arrau, the Chilean pianist, introduced them.

She was a petite blonde, slight but not frail, with somewhat the vibrant quality of Bernstein. Her name was Felicia Montealegre Cohn. Her father, Roy Cohn, was a West Coast engineer whose business had taken him to Costa Rica and Chile. Her great-grandfather had been a famous rabbi who founded San Francisco's Temple Emanu-El.

In Costa Rica, Roy Cohn had met and married Clemencia Montealegre. Later, the family had moved to Chile, and Felicia had grown up in the courtly old-world society of Santiago.

And what was she doing in New York? Felicia confessed she had practiced something of a deception on her family. She was stage-struck. But in Chile, well brought up young ladies did not go into the theater.

Felicia's solution had been to come to New York ostensibly for study with her friend and fellow-Chilean, Claudio Arrau. Music was, by Santiago standards, respectable.

Once on her own, however, she had let piano lessons go by the board. Her goal was the Broadway theater. And (she told Arrau after first meeting him) to marry Bernstein.

When Arrau laughed, she told him to wait and see.

That the electric shock of their first meeting had not been wholly one-sided was shown when, after the party, Bernstein asked to take her home.

Then, almost immediately, things began to go wrong.

Felicia, sharing a Greenwich Village apartment with another theater aspirant, had no telephone. Hence Bernstein could not reach her. From Rochester, where he had gone to conduct, Bernstein wired: "Telephone me." But he forgot to alert

Helen Coates, and his ever-vigilant secretary told Felicia the Maestro couldn't be disturbed.

Now this obviously was no way to get on with a proud Chilean beauty. The young lady's feelings were hurt.

Bernstein moreover was so overwhelmed by the sheer pressure of work as to have little time for courtship. Recalling their early, strained relationship, Felicia says today: "It was nip and tuck for a while."

Their first meeting took place in 1946. In 1947, their engagement was announced. It was broken off before the end of the year.

The two went their separate ways. Bernstein was off to his triumphs in Israel and his grand tour of European orchestras. For her part, Felicia, using her mother's maiden name as Felicia Montealegre, devoted herself to her career to such good effect that in 1950 she was named TV Actress of the Year.

It was at about this time that Bernstein was beginning to ask himself whether, for the time being, enough was not enough. For seven years, he had been traveling from podium to podium at a dead run. All his composing had been done in snatched moments of leisure. His newest score, incidental music for *Peter Pan*, opened at the Imperial Theater in July, 1950.

Almost immediately, he was off to Europe again,

playing the piano solo in his *Age of Anxiety* at Scheveningen, with Willem van Otterloo conducting the Hague Residentie Orchestra. As a diversion, there was a side trip to Donegal to visit Henry P. McIlhenny, curator of the Art Museum in Philadelphia. The Bernsteins, Leonard, Shirley, and Burton were fascinated by McIlhenny's authentic castle, which had fireplaces in every room but no electricity.

The holiday was blighted when the Bernstein brothers were incautious enough to go deer-stalking. They found it to be grimly serious work. They had not even been allowed to talk. The brothers returned at sundown. Both were pale and exhausted, and Leonard had fallen into a brook. For a long time thereafter, Shirley recalls, they were unnerved by the mention of deer-stalking.

Then, for Bernstein, back to the grind. In the spring of 1951, several dozen concerts later, he paused to take stock of his situation.

He had conducted nearly every orchestra in the world. And, as a perpetual guest conductor, he had had to face, as he put it, "a new orchestra every week."

There is no more exhausting way to make the Grand Tour. Every new orchestra is an unknown quantity. Orchestras, like people, have clearly defined personalities. These vary from nation to nation, even from city to city. Sir Thomas Beecham once disclosed (quoting racy examples) how in his long career he had built up files of jokes, some for use with French musicians, some for German, and some for British. Each new orchestra is a problem to solve.

Now Bernstein was tired of being an orchestral psychologist. He wanted to compose. Everything he had written thus far, except for early works like the clarinet sonata, had been done with his left hand, so to speak. He had composed under heavy time pressure, in the midst of many distractions. He had stolen time from performing and conducting to compose.

Now he was ready to unwind, to arrange his thoughts, to think back over the seven crowded years which had made him the most famous musician of his years in the world, to reflect on where he had been and where he was headed next.

Then, for once, he wanted a quiet place, free from distractions, in which to compose. A number of projects at the back of his mind were clamoring for attention.

Like every visitor to Mexico, Bernstein had been won by its breathtaking mountain scenery, mild year-round climate, smiling friendly people, and mellow Spanish-Colonial past. One was constantly meeting acquaintances like Martha Gellhorn, the writer.

Mexico, Bernstein decided, would be a good

resting place. A concert in Mexico City in the late spring of 1951 would be, for the time being, his last.

Miss Gellhorn knew just the place for Bernstein's sabbatical. In fact, she lived there herself. The place was Cuernavaca, a pleasant resort city famous for its association with the ill-starred Emperor Maximilian and his Empress Carlotta.

Bernstein went to Cuernavaca, liked what he saw, and rented a house with a swimming pool. On the first of June, 1951, sun-tanned, refreshed, and at peace with the world, he began writing an opera called *Trouble in Tahiti*.

Next day, he received a long-distance call from Boston. Koussevitzky was in the hospital.

"I had a dreadful feeling it was all over," Bernstein says. Without stopping to pack, he dashed to the Mexico City airport, landing in Boston twenty hours later.

In the hospital, on the night of his arrival, he had a long talk with Koussevitzky. They recalled triumphs they had shared, and disappointments as well.

Koussevitzky had looked on Bernstein as his successor with the B. S. O. When he had submitted his resignation, he had offered to rescind it if Bernstein were made co-conductor. Instead, the orchestra's directors had chosen to bring Charles Munch from Paris. This was a blow from which

Koussevitzky never quite recovered. In all his years with the orchestra, he had never had so flat a refusal before. "He got old that minute," Bernstein says.

It was late when Bernstein left the hospital. Next day, Koussevitzky died.

For Bernstein, as for Koussevitzky and the Tanglewood faculty, personal grief had to give way to the fact that the Tanglewood opening was less than a month away. Koussevitzky's death had left a big gap in the 1951 summer schedule. The festival could not carry on without a director. And that Koussevitzky wanted it to carry on there could be no doubt. He had spent a good deal of his time in his last years to just this purpose.

For the time being, at least, Bernstein was the logical man to take over. With a pang or two at the thought of his Cuernavaca hideaway and his unfinished opera, Bernstein set to work.

Those who were present still remember Bernstein's tribute to Koussevitzky at the opening concert that year. Reminding the Tanglewood students that eleven years earlier he, too, had been a student there, he exhorted them to carry on the Koussevitzky tradition by following "the central line, the line of mystery and fire, to be followed by dedicated people."

Few orchestras have ever played for Bernstein like the Tanglewood group. In August, he led a performance of the *Missa Solemnis* as a tribute to the memory of Koussevitzky. The eloquence of the performance, and the circumstances under which it was taking place, made an unforgettable occasion. At the "Kyrie," the "Gloria," and the "Credo," listeners could not refrain from applauding.

Was it loneliness at the death of his kindly mentor which led Bernstein to write a long letter to Felicia Montealegre? Even those concerned do not appear certain, except that Felicia Bernstein recalls that her future husband proposed to her, successfully, over dinner at Millbrook, New York, while they were driving up to Tanglewood.

Their engagement was announced by Mrs. Olga Koussevitzky at Tanglewood on August 12, 1951. They were married on September 9 in an Orthodox service at Bernstein's boyhood Temple Mishkan Tefila in Boston, and went to Mexico for their honeymoon.

During their journey, Bernstein discovered that his bride did not know what a past participle was. Shocked by this deficiency, he drilled her in grammar until she was reduced to tears.

Fortunately, Mrs. Bernstein is stable and possesses a sense of humor. Of this incident and others like it, she says: "Lenny *is* difficult to live with sometimes—but what man worth living with isn't?"

Back in Cuernavaca, the newlyweds relaxed in

the sun. That was where Constance Hope, the public relations counsel, found them when she and her husband motored to Mexico in December.

When they telephoned, Bernstein asked why they had not called earlier and come out to lunch. Miss Hope said the line had been busy.

"You know why it's been busy?" Bernstein replied. "We're pregnant."

Miss Hope immediately went into a shop and bought a pair of booties. She found the Bernsteins in white bathing suits, sitting by the pool "like the spirit of eternal youth."

"They looked at the booties and began to cry." Miss Hope says. "The present made the baby seem real."

Their life at Cuernavaca flowed by so pleasantly that they would have stayed indefinitely except for the baby. Bernstein felt he would be easier in his mind if the child were born in an American hospital.

Indecisive whether to go or stay, Bernstein's mind was made up by a distress call from the B. S. O. Charles Munch had had a heart attack. Would Bernstein put on his old school tie and hurry back to Boston? The Bernsteins boarded a plane for the United States.

Their daughter was born in New York on September 8, 1952. Marc Blitzstein asserted his right as godfather to suggest the name Nina, which was the heroine's name in an operetta he was then composing. The Bernsteins agreed.

Next morning, Bernstein called his wife at the hospital. "It's all a frightful mistake," he said. "Don't sign the papers."

If not Nina, then what?

"I have it," said Mrs. Bernstein. "Jamie."

"Why?"

"I don't know. I like it."

"I like it too."

"It makes no sense."

"Great!"

Chapter *12*

BERNSTEIN's rapidly expanding career took on still another dimension in June, 1952, when Brandeis University held its first commencement exercises.

The school, an experiment in Jewish sponsorship of non-sectarian education, had been founded in 1949 by leaders of the Greater Boston Jewish community, sparked largely by George Alpert, chairman of its board of trustees. Its name honored Louis Dembitz Brandeis, who had been a Boston lawyer before becoming a Justice of the U.S. Supreme Court.

As its first president, the young university chose Dr. Abram L. Sachar, former director of the Hillel Foundation. It took over the buildings and one-hundred-acre campus of Middlesex University, a defunct medical institution at Waltham and, in the best academic tradition, sent out a nation-wide appeal for funds.

Since Brandeis University had yet to graduate a class, the appeal went to "foster" alumni. A total of 36,000 women and 5,000 men responded. The university opened with four schools, those of Science, Social Service, Humanities, and Creative Arts.

The Creative Arts school was headed by Bernstein, who also occupied the Fredric and Sylvia Mann Chair in Music. It was endowed by Fredric R. Mann of Philadelphia, a paperboard manufacturer who, before attending the University of Pennsylvania's Wharton School of Finance, had studied piano with Rafael Joseffy at the Institute of Music Art, now part of the Juilliard School.

("No, I wasn't very talented," Mr. Mann says modestly. "I just practiced a lot.")

In retrospect, it seems clear that nobody, least of all Bernstein himself, expected him to spend five days a week lecturing on the Waltham campus.

On the other hand, Bernstein's indefatigable energy and his growing fame were academic assets. All schools prize faculty who perform or publish; in a dignified way, this is advertising almost as good as a winning football team.

The teaching idea appealed to Bernstein, who

already had shown evidence of the flair that would soon make him TV music-lecturer to the nation. And Brandeis University was a logical place for a man who had so firmly allied himself with Jewish causes and the Jewish community.

Bernstein's calm acceptance of his Jewishness in fact is in contrast to that of colleagues who have changed or abbreviated their names. It is said that Koussevitzky once urged him to adopt a more exotic name for professional purposes. His pupil would not hear of this. His name, he said, was Leonard Bernstein; what of it?

As his first big project, the Mann Professor of Music had planned a four-day Festival of the Creative Arts to be held in June, 1952, in conjunction with Brandeis University's first commencement exercises.

That the Festival (or the commencement, for that matter) actually took place was something of a marvel. Repair and construction of buildings was going on, campus roads were unpaved, and visitors floundered through mud to reach their destination. In his commencement address, Dr. Sachar noted that the canvas-topped amphitheater donated by Boston businessman Adolph Ullman, upon which work had started in February, had been unfinished at two o'clock on the afternoon of the first performance. It was ready, however, at curtain time.

Working feverishly at top speed, Bernstein had arranged a festival program which featured three important "firsts."

One was the Marc Blitzstein adaptation of Weill's *Threepenny Opera*, which would later have a long off-Broadway run.

Another was a composition by the French composer Pierre Schaeffer which gave U.S. listeners their first opportunity to hear *musique concrète,* in which street noises, bird calls and other sounds are tape recorded and combined in what the composer believes to be a musically meaningful design.

And finally there was the première of Bernstein's own one-act opera, *Trouble in Tahiti,* which despite the press of other duties he had somehow found time to complete.

Rounding out the festival were lively discussions of theater, films, the relation of music to society ("Do we really need or want the concert hall in the United States?"), in which Bernstein took a leading part.

Trouble in Tahiti did not please all listeners at its first hearing (what opera does?). Some felt that it sounded hastily written—which, of course, it was. It was certainly heard under unfavorable conditions at its première. Conceived as an intimate opera, it was wholly unsuited to performance in a large outdoor amphitheater. But Bernstein, like so many harassed artists before him, needed a new work in a hurry and this was the only one at hand. Later, *Trouble in Tahiti* was performed on television, at Tanglewood and, in April, 1955, on Broadway as part of *All in One*, which also included a one-act play by Tennessee Williams and dances by Paul Draper. It has had frequent performances by both amateur and professional groups.

In smaller settings, the irony dissipated in an outdoor amphitheater came through. The fatuous husband and bored housewife, watching an "escape" film about the South Seas, represented a return to the theme of *Facsimile*—the boredom and restlessness of people having no inner resource. The music again showed Bernstein's fluency in utilizing jazz idioms, and on the whole underscored the stage situation effectively.

The 1952 festival, besides being a personal triumph for Bernstein, had attracted so much attention and drawn so many visitors to the Brandeis campus that it was inevitable that it would be followed by another the following year.

The second festival, dedicated to "The Comic Spirit," featured an art exhibit, "Three Centuries of the Comic Spirit," and a new comedy, "The International Set," by Louis Kronenberger. Discussions on the cultural significance of the newspaper comic strip were led by Al Capp of "L'il Abner" and Milton Caniff, creator of "Terry and the Pirates." Humor in general was discussed by a panel which included the late Fred Allen, Irwin Corey, Arthur Kober, Alice Pearce, and S. J. Perelman. And comic poetry was appraised by David McCord, Ludwig Lewisohn, Newman Levy, and Earnest Hooton.

As its highlight, the second festival achieved a *coup* of considerable importance, the first U.S. performance of Francis Poulenc's opera, *Les mamelles de Tirésias.*

In the excitement of preparing the festivals, the Mann Professor did not neglect his classroom. Bernstein loves to teach — his TV lectures are, basically, brilliant pedagogy — and he is devoted to the cause of Brandeis.

In his first academic year, he made weekly or at least semiweekly trips to Waltham to conduct two courses. One was a general lecture, followed by a question-and-answer period, which was open to all interested students. The other was a stiff course in composition, limited to graduate students at masters' level.

Both classes were hugely successful; but coming on top of all his other commitments, they left Bernstein exhausted. The trip to Waltham was both arduous and time-consuming; it was, he says, "like three days of the week gone."

For his second year, he tried a new plan, visiting the Brandeis campus only once a month, but remaining several days.

This season was even more successful than the first. Students who were in his classes still talk of such stimulating experiences as guest lectures by Lillian Hellman and other theater personalities; of hearing Marc Blitzstein's newly composed *Regina* played and sung by Bernstein and the composer.

Bernstein was by this time deep in *Candide,* and fascinated his composition students by discussing with them the problems which he encountered. As a composition assignment, he set them to work solving the same problems.

But Bernstein, always the perfectionist, on assessing his course at the end of the year found it to have been inadequate. His visits to the university were, it is true, even more of an event when they took place monthly than they had been at weekly intervals. But in the long stretches between, students were, as Bernstein puts it, "deprived of continuity." It was not easy to pick up where they had left off.

Bernstein felt this to be unfair to his students, although there is no record that the students thought so.

At any rate, seeing no way to resolve the difficulties of commuting to Brandeis, Bernstein at the end of his second academic year asked for and obtained leave of absence. To his great regret, it has continued ever since.

"It's perfectly possible to do all the things I have to do," he observed, "but it's a little hard doing them all at once."

One can sympathize with the hard-pressed man of many talents. On the other hand, the complications are sometimes of his own making.

Such a complication occurred in the fall of 1952, when, after the first Brandeis festival and the Tanglewood season, Bernstein had resumed his fall round of activity.

About a year earlier, the Comden-Green-Bernstein talent pool had been approached to do a musical. *My Sister Eileen*, originally a series of *New Yorker* short stories, had been a hit when turned into a play. So the obvious next step was to set it to music.

Bernstein and his colleagues discussed the idea, but couldn't see it. *My Sister Eileen,* they felt, just would not make a musical.

Producers Fryer and Carr thereupon engaged another composer and lyricist to do the score, and signed Rosalind Russell as the star.

Matters went on by fits and starts, in the time-honored manner of the Broadway theater, until six weeks before the opening date specified in Miss Russell's contract. Then the producers made the horrifying discovery that they "had no show." The score simply did not work. And a musical with a defective score is obviously doomed from the start.

A desperate SOS went out to Comden and Green. They, in turn, approached Bernstein.

"Look," they said, "basically we're all not very much interested in doing this show. But the producers are in a jam. How about it?"

The gifted man thought it over. As usual, he had projects enough to keep him busy. But *My Sister Eileen* represented a challenge, something from which Bernstein has never been known to back away. To allow a minimum of two weeks of rehearsals, the score would have to be finished in four weeks—an obvious impossibility. It was so obviously impossible that Bernstein ended by saying he would do it.

The Bernsteins were living, as they still do, in a big apartment on West Fifty-seventh Street. On another floor is Bernstein's studio, painted dull gray and lighted entirely by artificial light to keep distraction at a minimum. Bernstein's name for it is his "thinking room." Miss Comden calls it "Lenny's cave."

The collaborators sat there, telling each other how little enthusiasm they felt for *My Sister Eileen*. It was dated. Many of its once topical allusions had become passé. It was, as Adolph Green put it, "thirties-bound."

"The thirties!" Bernstein exclaimed. "My God, those were the years! The excitement that was around! The political awareness! The optimism! Franklin Delano! Fiorello! Real personalities! And the songs! Remember the songs?"

He rushed to the piano and played one, and another. Then he said, "Say, I've got a great idea for a *Sister Eileen* song."

He did have, too. And one idea sparked another. The collaborators were off. They spent the next four weeks in the "thinking room," the air so blue with cigarette smoke that, Miss Comden recalls, "we could hardly see each other."

Anxious listeners outside the door observed their progress. As each number was finished, Miss Russell would say: "O.K., geniuses, let's have it."

Broadway observers are not certain whether this did or did not set a record for putting together the score of a musical. In any case, *Wonderful Town* opened at the Winter Garden on February 25, 1953, meeting the terms of Miss Russell's contract. It ran for five hundred and fifty-three performances, winning the Drama Critics Award as the year's best musical, and Bernstein's score received the Antoinette Perry and Donaldson awards. It had been a good four weeks' work.

Chapter 13

For BERNSTEIN, *Wonderful Town* was a brief interlude in his endless round of composing and conducting engagements. One of the latter was a guest appearance with the New York Philharmonic at which he led the first complete performance of Charles Ives's Second Symphony. Composed many years earlier, it had lain neglected while conductors passed on to works posing fewer difficulties for listeners and performers.

Not all conductors are drawn to contemporary works. Toscanini made no secret of the fact that he did not understand the new music, did not like it, and was content to leave its interpretation to younger men. Those who played under Toscanini also noted his tendency to be thrown off, although only momentarily, by odd or erratic time signatures.

Ives, the rugged Connecticut individualist, who supported his art by running an insurance agency, took delight in strewing his scores with difficulties, such as a passage in which the conductor must beat four-in-a-bar with one hand and three with the other. Some of his works, in particular the songs, are difficult to the point of being unperformable. When this was pointed out, Ives's reply was, "What of it?" He was perfectly content to have his music exist only on paper or, as he put it, "in the leaf."

It is small wonder that Ives performances have been infrequent.

For Bernstein, however, the Ives symphony proved to be a congenial task. He has a genuine flair for contemporary music, that of other composers as well as his own. This cannot be said of every conductor. Today's music has so far departed from traditional style that Bach, Beethoven, Brahms, and Mozart no longer furnish reliable precedent. As one harassed conductor put it, "When you begin to rehearse a modern score, you never know *what* will come out, do you?"

Bernstein knows. His sure-handedness in this area of music is remarkable. It is possible to quarrel—as some do—with his interpretation of a Mozart symphony, but his severest detractors admit that in putting together a difficult contemporary score he is nothing less than a whiz.

Bernstein had another opportunity to display

this flair in March, 1953, when at Town Hall he led an orchestra assembled for the occasion in a concert honoring the tenth anniversary of the Koussevitzky Foundation. Works heard at the concert, all commissioned by the Foundation, were a mixed lot. There was a first U.S. performance of *Tartiniana*, by the Italian twelve-tone composer Dallapiccola; a modest, romantic *Prelude for Orchestra* by Edward Burlingame Hill; Nikolai Lopatnikoff's *Concertino for Orchestra*, and Harold Shapero's *Symphony for Classical Orchestra*.

Bernstein was doing what he has done consistently all through his career—lending a hand to the contemporary composer. In his gloomy moments, he is inclined to wonder why the helping hand is not reciprocated. Bernstein is a contemporary composer, too. But his works are seldom played by others.

It seems to be generally true that, given a choice of a Bernstein work and a composition by someone less famous and less successful, the other man gets the nod. As one colleague put it, "Lenny is the one young American composer who doesn't need help."

And it must be admitted that he has a point. As composer-conductor, Bernstein virtually has his choice of the world's great orchestras for a showcase. (He has, however, shown restraint in programing his own compositions.)

Bernstein moreover has an affinity for artistic ventures which are also commercially profitable— which strikes more ivory-towered artists as almost indecent.

One such assignment was writing music for the film, *On the Waterfront*. Although this was Bernstein's first venture in Hollywood, it was successful enough to be nominated for an Academy Award.

In December, 1953, Bernstein added to his string of firsts that of being the first American-born, American-trained conductor to lead opera at world-famous La Scala in Milan.

For Bernstein, the performance was a memorable new opportunity. Although he had had little previous operatic experience, aside from conducting the U.S. première of *Peter Grimes* at Tanglewood in 1947, like nearly all conductors he was fascinated by opera. Reiner once stated the reason cogently: "There are so many more things that can go wrong." In a concert, one has only the orchestra to worry about. At the opera, singers can forget lines, scenery can collapse, gowns can snag on projecting nails, performers even die on the stage. Conducting opera can be unpredictable.

Another complication of Bernstein's La Scala debut was that it was to be made conducting a revival of Cherubini's infrequently heard *Medea*, with brilliant, stormy Maria Callas in the title role.

Bernstein's debut in *Medea* came about because of the indisposition of Victor de Sabata, who had originally been scheduled to conduct. It was a measure of Bernstein's growing international stature as a conductor that La Scala, passing over numbers of available conductors, urged him to replace De Sabata.

Bernstein replied, reasonably enough, that he had come to Italy to lead concerts, not opera; that he had little operatic experience; and that he did not know a single note of *Medea*.

But La Scala's representatives were not to be put off. From Milan, they followed him to Florence, where he had gone to conduct, and again met with a refusal. Undaunted, they pursued him to Rome.

Finally, Bernstein said he would do it. By now, the negotiations had consumed so much time that he had exactly five days to prepare a performance of a work he did not know.

Had Bernstein fully realized what he was getting into, it might have daunted even this veteran of many tight squeezes.

The Scala audience was split into two hostile factions, the Callas party and that of Renata Tebaldi. These were not a claque, as is sometimes erroneously reported—at La Scala, as at the Metropolitan, the claque is a group of quiet, unobtrusive professionals—but noisy partisans, eager for an excuse to stage a demonstration. As would be the case at the Metropolitan later on, Tebaldi fans would have loved nothing more than to see Callas fall flat in an important role, and the other way around.

The year before, La Scala had avoided friction by engaging Callas for the first half of the season, Tebaldi for the last. Now the audacious plan was for Tebaldi to open the season in a revival of Catalani's *La Wally*, with Callas's *Medea* the following night.

Meanwhile, Bernstein, miserable with bronchitis, was up to his eyebrows in *Medea*. The score from which he learned the music was a musty antique, giving off clouds of dust to which Bernstein proved violently allergic. Wheezing and sneezing, he began with the orchestra his exploration of the Cherubini score, deciding where to make cuts, looking for passages where trouble could be expected, and so on.

"We [the orchestra] learned the music together," he recalls.

In many ways, *Medea* was the most audacious feat Bernstein had yet attempted. Aside from the inherently greater complexity of operatic versus orchestral performance, he was dealing with an unfamiliar score, an Italian-speaking orchestra and a prima donna tagged in all the world's opera houses as "difficult"—all this in a situation made explosive by the rivalry of the Callas-Tebaldi fan clubs.

Bernstein's flair for foreign languages, of which he now speaks five, solved the communications problem. And he hit it off immediately with Callas. In her, he found a temperament in many ways like his own. Even those who dislike Callas concede that she is a tireless perfectionist who will rehearse thirteen hours without stopping to achieve a desired effect. In her own way, she is as much a dynamo of energy as Bernstein in his. The two understood and respected each other.

Excitement mounted as opening night approached —so much so that the Milanese critic Emilio Radius suggested that Callas and Tebaldi ought to have a public reconciliation for the greater glory of La Scala. Callas took the hint and on opening night was conspicuously seated in a box, applauding heartily for Tebaldi.

The following night, Tebaldi did not appear.

The *Medea* performance was the pay-off. The Milanese take opera seriously. Even favorites may be hissed on an off night. But for *Medea*, they stood and cheered. From the first note, it was obvious that the conductor had matters firmly in hand. At the final curtain, Bernstein shared half a dozen bows with Callas. The verdict of the *Corriere della Sera* was that the performance was "indisputably brilliant."

Toscanini's daughter, the Countess Castelbarco, had privately communicated her forebodings to the Maestro. Bernstein had been incredibly rash to undertake so staggering a project at short notice. He would be scalped, slaughtered, roasted alive.

After the performance, the Countess had the pleasure of retracting. In all her years in Milan, she could not remember so spectacular a triumph.

It was all the more welcome because only a short time had elapsed since the late Leonard Warren, at the height of his powers and singing his greatest role, had had a surprisingly cool reception in La Scala's *Rigoletto*. Some ascribed it to a performance which, aside from Warren's singing of the title role, was poorly prepared. Others blamed an upsurge of anti-American sentiment.

At any rate, *Medea* redressed the balance handsomely.

Bernstein now found that he had a new love—opera. He was fascinated by its pitfalls and possibilities. Operatic repertoire was a whole new world which he was bursting with eagerness to explore.

But, as usual, the great problem was how to find the time. Other projects would soon be clamoring more urgently for his attention. Opera would have to yield precedence to "The Orchestra That Would Not Die."

Chapter *14*

IN THE FALL OF 1937, Samuel Chotzinoff, then music critic of the New York *Post* and an intimate friend of Toscanini, found himself in Milan on a delicate diplomatic mission. It was to persuade the Maestro to lead an orchestra especially created for him by the National Broadcasting Company.

The plan represented a farsighted public relations concept on the part of NBC officials, and of David Sarnoff, president of the parent Radio Corporation of America, in particular.

The basic reason for undertaking so costly a project was the somewhat anomalous position of radio-TV in the press-communications world. Radio-TV, unlike the newspapers, must take into account not only public opinion but the Federal

Communications Commission, which by not renewing licenses could, in theory at least, wipe out the networks overnight. In all their squabbles with the FCC, the networks have not pressed the issue to a final showdown. Radio-TV has not yet had its John Peter Zenger, and nobody is anxious to be first.

Hence a certain timidity about controversial issues on the part of the networks. (This is galling to newspapers, who sometimes find themselves fighting radio-TV's battles in the interest of freedom of the press, while at the same time losing great chunks of advertising revenue to this upstart medium.)

Hence, too, the networks' tendency to stress their public service functions. It would certainly be a public service to provide great music, freely available at the flip of a dial. And NBC would trump Columbia's ace, the Sunday Philharmonic broadcasts, with an orchestra especially created for the most renowned of living conductors.

Toscanini heard the proposal with mixed emotions. He pointed out that he was old; that he had been conducting for more than forty years; that he had just completed ten strenuous years with the New York Philharmonic.

On the other hand, he was openly out of sympathy with the Fascist regime, which had just created an international scandal by withholding his passport. As early as 1931, he had been beaten up by Fascists in Bologna following his refusal to conduct the Fascist anthem.

Toscanini at length agreed. NBC immediately set the wheels in motion, engaging Artur Rodzinski as drillmaster to conduct preliminary auditions and whip the orchestra into shape. On Christmas night, 1937, Toscanini raised his baton and began seventeen more years of music-making, spanning some of the most memorable performances of his career.

"Quando in mano mi trema la bacchetta, non farò più il direttore," Toscanini once told a friend. *"Ma quel tempo non è ancora giunto."*

But the time did come, the baton did tremble, and in April, 1954, the NBC Symphony found itself leaderless and disbanded.

Its members, having recovered from their initial shock, stubbornly resolved that the organization built by years of dogged work under Toscanini ought somehow to be kept together. As Toscanini's orchestra, they were the equals, they felt, of the Philharmonic any day.

Support, moral and financial, came from many sources. Once again, the question was raised of why New York could not support more than a single orchestra. Don Gillis, who had been producer of the NBC Symphony broadcasts, took a leading part in forming the non-profit corporation

165

which set up headquarters in Carnegie Hall and announced that the orchestra would carry on as The Symphony of the Air.

The orchestra played a Carnegie Hall concert with a spotlight trained on the vacant podium. It also recorded a twelve-inch LP disk, copies of which were sent to anyone contributing ten dollars or more to the orchestra's treasury.

But nobody really expected the Symphony of the Air to function permanently as a conductorless orchestra. Such an experiment had failed both here and in Russia. What the Symphony of the Air needed in a hurry was (a) money and (b) a permanent conductor.

Bernstein then had no orchestra and the Symphony of the Air no conductor. Their mutual affinity was evident.

In the reorganized orchestra's first season, Bernstein made several appearances as its guest conductor. Among other things, he conducted it in a Hanukkah Festival at Madison Square Garden, with Jennie Tourel and Jan Peerce as soloists. His earliest *Omnibus* telecasts were made with the Symphony of the Air. In the orchestra's 1955-56 season he led it in a series of six concerts at Carnegie Hall.

At exactly what point Bernstein's relations with the Symphony of the Air began to cool, it is now

166

difficult to say. But his guest appearances grew less frequent, and finally stopped altogether.

What happened?

One version is so firmly established in the folklore of Fifty-seventh Street as to be worth mentioning. When the Symphony of the Air made its decision to go ahead on its own, it had, simply as a matter of getting things done, to have a business manager to handle money and sign contracts, someone else to decide artistic policy, someone to take care of publicity, and all the other details which go into the planning of an orchestral season. Gillis could not handle everything, and after a time the press of other duties forced him to leave the Symphony of the Air altogether.

Consequently, the orchestra entrusted its affairs to a board of directors elected from its own membership. David Walter, a double-bass player, presided at the board room table, contributed by an admirer, around which the board of directors conducted its deliberations.

The idea of musicians functioning as a board of directors tickled the fancy of the late Meyer Berger, then writing his "About New York" column in the New York *Times*. As soon as he could contrive to do so, Berger dropped in at a board session to see what was going on.

As the musical fates would have it, he found

167

the board members, some with their feet placed thoughtfully on the table, considering what to do about a forthcoming concert of Italian music, with Bernstein conducting and with Renata Tebaldi and Jussi Bjoerling as soloists; and a later performance with Jennie Tourel.

"The main problem," Berger reported in the *Times*, of December 12, 1955, "was a rehearsal hall for the December 20 concert. Mr. Bjoerling, it seemed, could not leave Chicago until December 15. Rehearsal halls are almost all taken during holiday season.

"The board kicked that subject around, and in talky crossfire decided that 'Lenny' (Mr. Bernstein) would have to be persuaded that a Vivaldi number would throw the all-Italian opera show off balance.

"Leon Frengut, viola, quietly suggested bits from Rossini—ballet numbers from 'William Tell,' for example, instead of Vivaldi. Alan Shulman, 'cello, liked that. Undirectorially, he hummed snatches of Rossini ballets, and the faces around the table lighted. Lenny's Vivaldi went out the window, with never a formal 'aye' or 'nay.'"

After this item appeared in Meyer Berger's column, Bernstein's appearances with the Symphony of the Air became less frequent and finally stopped. Musical gossip said this was not entirely coincidence.

168

Bernstein's recollection of the incident is a bit different. He hoots at the foregoing one as "nonsense." He read—and was entertained by—Berger's account of the board meeting, but that was not the reason why his appearances with the Symphony of the Air dwindled and finally ceased.

The prosaic fact was that Bernstein had his hands full. So many other projects were clamoring for his attention as to leave little time for what was essentially a philanthropic undertaking. He had conducted, when asked, to help the orchestra establish itself on its new, independent footing. (And the orchestra, by the way, was glad to have the demonstrated pulling power of his name at the box office, in preference to those of other conductors who were eager to lead the Symphony of the Air.)

As for being the orchestra's permanent conductor, Bernstein maintains that this idea was never seriously discussed and that, if it had been, he would have quashed it. At that time, he says, he had no wish to tie himself to a permanent orchestral post. His three years with the New York City Symphony had shown him how great a burden of administrative detail, even in the relatively brief New York City Symphony season, fell on the conductor's shoulders. In an orchestral post continuing through the winter, he would have no time whatever to call his own. And there were, as usual, several big projects on which he was eager to begin working.

This, according to Bernstein, is the true story of his parting with the Symphony of the Air.

Another story which, Bernstein says, has improved with re-telling is that of how he was *not* offered the San Francisco Symphony.

According to this bit of musical gossip, when Bernstein was invited to San Francisco it was ostensibly just another of his many guest-conducting engagements. In reality, he was being looked over as a possible successor to Pierre Monteux. The octogenarian conductor had announced that he no longer felt up to the strain of a winter season, and wished to limit himself to guest engagements and his summer conducting school in Maine.

But Bernstein, according to report, did not please conservative San Francisco tastes. Too "choreographic," perhaps. San Franciscans were accustomed to the economical beat of Monteux, whose reduction of conducting to absolute minimum essentials made Reiner seem almost flamboyant. Not Bernstein, but Enrique Jorda was Monteux's successor.

Bernstein's comment on this is that if San Francisco regarded his guest engagement as a sort of audition, he for his part did not look at it that way.

All through the early stages of his career, he maintains, he had resisted permanent appointments insofar as was possible. He had tried, unsuccessfully, to talk Koussevitzky out of making his joint-conductorship proposal to the Boston Symphony Orchestra, and was on the whole relieved when it was refused. He had taken over the New York City Symphony when the venture seemed on the point of collapsing, and for the next three seasons had written little. Thereafter he was happy to limit himself to guest engagements, since even these left him scant time for composition.

Had so flattering an offer as San Francisco been made, Bernstein cannot, of course, say with finality that he would not have accepted. But on the whole he is inclined to doubt it. Even when offered the orchestra which no conductor in the world would have refused, he did a great deal of soul-searching before consenting to take it.

Chapter 15

TELEVISION, although broadcast on a more or less regular schedule as early as the New York World's Fair of 1939, did not really come into its own until after World War II. Prior to that time, there were not enough receiving sets to interest advertisers; and the networks, with millions tied up in the new medium, sought to fill air time as cheaply as possible with commercial documentary movies and similar "canned" material.

Then, suddenly, as it had for radio in the thirties, the Golden Age dawned, and video, its pockets crammed with money, found itself looking about for new talent and new ideas.

Almost from the first, it was recognized that orchestral concerts were a good TV prospect. It was recognized, too, that orchestras presented special problems for the camera. There was just so much that could be done in the way of training cameras on strings or woodwinds for important solo passages. The symphony orchestra, so absorbing a spectacle in the concert hall, with its strings bowing splendidly in unison, or bowing splendidly out of unison, Philadelphia Orchestra style, was for video purposes just a bit static. Seeing the orchestra perform added little to the pleasure of hearing it on the radio.

What was needed was a new idea, a photogenic conductor, and a sponsor who was not afraid to experiment. All these elements came together in the famous *Omnibus* telecast of November 14, 1954, which firmly established Bernstein as a nationally known TV personality.

It was a daring break with the proved if overworked formulas of Westerns, murder mysteries, and situation comedies. "Nobody knew whether people would sit still for forty-five minutes on a subject like this," Bernstein recalls. But *Omnibus* was willing to gamble forty-five minutes of air time to find out.

It could have been deadly. Few things are duller than a dull music-appreciation lecture. But whatever Bernstein's shortcomings, dullness is not one of them. The Beethoven lecture made an entertaining telecast and, as later edited for publication, is a delightfully readable passage in Bernstein's *The Joy of Music*.

Bernstein is quick to point out that the Beethoven telecast was the product of many minds and hands. There were, however, unmistakable Bernsteinian touches all through, such as his description of musical form as not being a mold for Jello but a road map for the composer's spiritual journey. Bernstein has a flair for illustrations of this kind, which are homely, apt, and make the point clear in a flash.

And Bernstein's special contribution was one which made all the difference. What, after all, could be said about the Beethoven Fifth Symphony that was new? One could hardly get through the U.S. public school system without hearing its famous opening quoted as an example of a "theme."

Bernstein's touch of genius was in coming up with a fresh idea.

Most music-lovers know in a general way about the Beethoven sketchbooks, in which the composer jotted down music ideas as they occurred to him, and laboriously polished and reshaped them. Many of the sketches are published in Thayer's *Life of Beethoven*, if one has the strength to plow through Thayer's three copious volumes.

How would it be, asked Bernstein, if they went back to preliminary versions of the symphony's opening movement, showing what the Fifth Symphony would have sounded like if Beethoven's

174

tireless quest for perfection had not made him discard each good version for a better one?

That was how it was done, conveying better than any lengthy essay a sense of the furious struggle with stubborn musical materials out of which the Beethoven symphonies were wrought.

The Beethoven telecast was a great artistic success. Television reviewers, outspokenly concerned about the low average quality of TV fare, were delighted. But what staggered Bernstein, *Omnibus*, and CBS was the public response.

The show had appealed to all sorts of listeners, musically knowledgeable and otherwise. "We got letters from plumbers and professors, little children and old men," says Bernstein.

A CBS wag theorized that women viewers were drawn by Bernstein's sex appeal, men by his persuasive salesmanship.

"He appeals to youngsters," said an assistant producer, "because he looks and acts completely normal, doesn't patronize them, and can also be very funny."

Most gratifying of all was that musicians liked Bernstein on TV. They, perhaps better than anyone else, realized that Bernstein had resisted the temptation to over-simplify. Certainly his was not the widely held conception of the radio-TV audience as possessing the collective mentality of a three-year-old. He presupposed on the part of his hearers some knowledge to start with, curiosity to learn more, and sufficient attention span to follow his explanation to the end.

"You get the feeling that Lenny is talking to you as an equal," one musician said, "and that he respects your intelligence."

"Even if I disagreed with what Lenny says, which I don't," said another performer, "I'd be all for him just on account of the interest he creates in music."

A television lecture as successful as the *Omnibus* Beethoven had to be followed by another. It took place on October 16, 1955, and explored "The World of Jazz." Again, Bernstein showed his knack of finding just the right simile to describe a technical aspect of music—for example, his description of syncopation as being like a missed heartbeat.

A month and a half later, on December 4, 1955, his *Omnibus* telecast was devoted to "The Art of Conducting." In a manner which must have gratified his old master Fritz Reiner, Bernstein explained that the first beat in a bar is always down and the last is up, showed how to vary the beat in order to convey the effect of staccato, legato, a broad sustained line, or a playful scherzo, and introduced watchers to the mysteries of reading a full score.

All these technical matters, Bernstein pointed out, were the elementary ABC's of the conductor's craft. He next considered "the intangibles, the deep magical aspect of conducting."

In all the literature of the period in which full-fledged conductors have existed—that is, from the early nineteenth century to the present—the conductor's function has not often been more interestingly summed up than in the passage in which Bernstein describes the qualities of the really great conductor.

And this summing-up would have been beyond the powers of many older, more experienced men. Bernstein is articulate; some conductors are not.

Koussevitzky, though intensely receptive to music, was so inarticulate he often could not make his meaning clear to a trained group of professional musicians. And for Toscanini, conducting was something to do, not to philosophize about. When aspiring conductors wrote to him for advice, the Maestro's response was invariably the same. *"Mon Dieu,"* he would exclaim in his croaky voice, "the way to learn conducting is to conduct."

It is difficult to picture either Koussevitzky or Toscanini, with all their gifts, presenting an *Omnibus* lecture.

Nor does Bernstein present them except on *Omnibus*. There must be a certain amount of talk at a rehearsal, he has pointed out, since there are things that cannot be explained by gesture alone. But long speeches about music for the benefit of musicians are a waste of time. Admirers of his polished TV delivery might be jolted at rehearsal to hear Bernstein ask for a passage played *"sehr* square" or "not rubato—just relaxo." But the musicians understand what he means.

The response to Bernstein's *Omnibus* telecast on conducting dwarfed all that had gone before. Astonished CBS officials were ready to swear that the nation was full of frustrated conductors, eager to conduct phonograph records in front of a mirror if they only knew how. It was soon after this telecast that a recording of "Music for Frustrated Conductors," complete with baton, appeared in the record shops.

An "Introduction to Modern Music" on January 13, 1957, showed how far Bernstein had progressed from the Boston youngster inventing his own terminology for tonic, subdominant, and dominant chords. The mature Bernstein had a thorough mastery of tonality, which he explained in terms of a baseball diamond, with the tonic as "home plate." His lucid exposition of the aims and purposes of modern music, the schools into which it is divided, and the direction each is taking, must have clarified many listeners' understanding of a musical idiom often considered baffling.

For many viewers, the Bach telecast of March 31,

1957, was one of the outstanding ones. Starting from the basic premise that most of his listeners found Bach pretty boring and that that was nothing to be ashamed of, Bernstein sneaked up on his audience with so masterly a piece of salesmanship as to be irresistible. There is no telling how many new friends the telecast made for the music of Bach, but their number must have been considerable.

Bernstein's *Omnibus* lectures abounded in clever touches, like rewriting Beethoven's Fifth Symphony, or having musicians stand on an enormously oversize page of the score to show the composition of Beethoven's orchestra; or, in his opera lecture, having a scene from *La Boheme* alternately spoken by actors and performed by singers. Basically, however, they were soundly based musical lectures, as learned as they were witty, with a solid foundation of knowledge. The special gift which Bernstein demonstrated, and which charmed his listeners, was that of turning a familiar idea topsy-turvy, so to speak, to examine it from a fresh point of view.

His *Omnibus* series established Bernstein firmly as a TV personality. In a recent season, watchers of his eight programs over CBS-TV totaled well over 75,000,000.

He was in fact so well established that TV comedians began building skits around "Leonard

Burnside," an erudite but twitchy young man who lectures on Beethoven's Fifth Symphony. "It opens with three G's," one "Burnside" lecture began. "Of course, I got more than that for doing this show."

Bernstein is vastly entertained by the skits, except when they are flat and pointless. Everyone knows what imitation is the sincerest form of. Also, the skits are based on the not unflattering assumption that a nation-wide TV audience will recognize the original whom they parody. Hence the original does not distress himself when comedians make jokes about "Leonard Burnside."

Chapter 16

Two things made the 1955-56 season memorable for the Bernsteins—the birth on July 7, 1955, of a son honoring the memory of Koussevitzky with his name of Alexander Serge, and a new turning point in Bernstein's career which would eventually lead to the conductorship of the New York Philharmonic.

The Philharmonic has been called with some justice "the graveyard of conductors." It is a superb group of professionals. Man for man, its players cannot be outclassed anywhere. On the other hand, a more cynical, hard-bitten body of musicians is not to be found. They do their best in performances, because that is the musician's instinct; but they are past masters at hazing conductors and utterly merciless to anyone who shows the slightest sign of weakness.

One of the most proficient hecklers was Bruno Labate, the Philharmonic's five-foot-tall oboist who boasted that he had $60,000 in the bank and feared no conductor alive. When guest conductor Otto Klemperer lectured the orchestra at what Labate considered excessive length, the diminutive oboist cut him short with: "Mista Klemps, you talk-a too much."

Guido Cantelli, Toscanini's brilliant, sensitive protégé, hated the Philharmonic and on occasion at rehearsals was reduced to tears. An ironic touch was that the plane in which he was killed was bringing him back for the dreaded chore of leading the Philharmonic. Stokowski is on record with respect to the orchestra: "Never again." And Koussevitzky once explained to a younger colleague his reason for not appearing with the New York orchestra: "My boy, dey are bendits."

One reason for this state of affairs is the sheer rigor of the Philharmonic season. No other orchestra in America has to face the fierce glare of publicity which beats upon the Philharmonic. The orchestra is overworked and over-reviewed. And, whereas in nearly every other city the hard facts about a bad performance are tempered by realization that this is, after all, the home team, the Philharmonic can expect no such lenient "constructive criticism." New York is the musical capital, and the only acceptable standard for the Philharmonic is to play better than anybody else.

Another factor unsettling the Philharmonic was the constant reshuffling of conductors. If Bernstein in his early barnstorming days found it exhausting to adjust to a new orchestra every week, an orchestra faces similar difficulties in adjusting to a constant procession of new conductors. Recent history appears to indicate that orchestras flourish best under the regular tenure of a Koussevitzky or Munch in Boston, a Stokowski or Ormandy in Philadelphia.

The Philharmonic if anything went to the other extreme. In the twenties and thirties, it offered, in addition to its chief luminary, Toscanini, such guest conductors as Igor Stravinsky, Arthur Honegger, Clemens Krauss, Fritz Reiner, Ossip Gabrilowitsch, Bernardino Molinari, Erich Kleiber, Issay Dobrowen, Sir Thomas Beecham, Ottorino Respighi, Leopold Stokowski, Hans Lange, Bruno Walter, Werner Janssen, Otto Klemperer, Artur Rodzinski, Carlos Chavez, Georges Enesco, and John Barbirolli. It was a constant, dazzling parade of talent, as if the Philharmonic feared subscribers would become bored looking at the same old faces.

(To this school of thought, Richard Burgin's tart reply is that music is for listening, not watching.)

It has been said of Toscanini that throughout his long career, he left a trail of demoralized orchestras behind him. He certainly left one in the Philharmonic when, in 1936, after ten years of superb music-making, he resigned.

As his successor, the Philharmonic chose a young Englishman who had made a good impression the previous season.

The subsequent career which earned him knighthood has shown Sir John Barbirolli to be by no means an undistinguished conductor. Unfortunately, he was not the right man for the Philharmonic after Toscanini. It is possible that no one would have been.

Barbirolli's youth and relative inexperience were handicaps, too. By 1940, it was apparent that the Philharmonic's playing—and morale—had deteriorated badly. When Barbirolli's contract expired, it was not renewed.

Then began a period of guest conductorships. The Philharmonic, like a mettlesome steed, chafed, fretted, and on occasion nearly unhorsed its riders. Something had to be done.

It was, with the appointment of Artur Rodzinski as musical director in 1943.

Rodzinski, gruff and short-tempered, was known as a "difficult" conductor. He had left orchestral posts in Philadelphia, Los Angeles, and Cleveland after squabbles in which he charged management with bad faith.

On the other hand, he was famous as a drillmaster and iron disciplinarian. He was the very man to cope with a brilliant, sulky orchestra which, it was felt, had gotten out of hand.

The prescription worked, more or less, until February, 1947. At that point, Rodzinski walked out on his $56,000-a-year job, charging managerial "interference" in selection of soloists and planning of programs. Management retorted that by programing such expensive features as big works for chorus, soloists, and orchestra he had put the Philharmonic budget even more out of balance than normal.

While the controversy, joyfully reported in detail by the press, was raging, there was the problem of a successor. Bruno Walter, though unwilling to assume the burden of full responsibility, carried on for two seasons as musical adviser and principal conductor. In the fall of 1949, Dimitri Mitropoulos, who had had considerable success with the Minneapolis Symphony, arrived to share a season with Stokowski. The next season, Mitropoulos was named musical director.

The Mitropoulos era was a colorful page in Philharmonic history. It soon became apparent that Mitropoulos was a brilliant but erratic leader.

He did certain types of music, contemporary works in particular, superlatively well. With Haydn, Mozart, the three B's and other standard repertoire, results were sometimes less happy.

By 1955, Mitropoulos had had a heart attack, and the lure of his first love, opera, was becoming too powerful to ignore. It was announced that for the following season, 1956-57, he would share the burden with two "chief guests," Paul Paray and Leonard Bernstein.

A year later, the Philharmonic announced that Bernstein had been engaged as co-director of the orchestra, beginning with the 1957-58 season.

Bernstein meanwhile was asking himself what all this was leading to. He had not sought a permanent post, in fact had resisted it in order to have time for composing. Now he found himself committed to the Philharmonic and the signs were plain that he might succeed Mitropoulous as musical director.

Bernstein was not sure he wanted it. Since 1943, he had had intimate, backstage knowledge of the Philharmonic's affairs. He had a very good idea of the pressures, of all kinds, to which its conductor was subjected. Going over in his mind the list of older, more experienced men who had come to grief in the "conductors' graveyard," he asked himself how he could expect to succeed in bringing it off.

Moreover, the Philharmonic tradition in conductors was European. If he were to head the orchestra, he would be its first American-born, American-trained conductor since the days of Ureli Corelli Hill, another Bostonian who was its founder-conductor in 1842. He would be, next to Barbirolli, its youngest conductor. And his association with the Broadway theater could be expected to make him suspect in the eyes of conservative Philharmonic subscribers.

At this point, Felicia Bernstein asserted her wifely right to tell him he was wrong. Everything he had done, she pointed out, had been directly or indirectly preparing him for the Philharmonic. And, for its part, a young, vigorous American conductor was just what the Philharmonic needed. Bernstein was not to fret, but cross his Philharmonic bridges when he came to them.

Bernstein knew she was right. One simply could not turn down the New York Philharmonic without giving it a try. If the call came, he would accept.

It did; and in fifteen years, not long as time goes, Bernstein had made it from untried debutant to conductor of the nation's number one orchestra.

Once his appointment was announced, Bernstein began to have misgivings. Many obstacles loomed ahead, giving him at times a sense of having bitten off more than he could chew.

A particular hazard was his first meeting with the board of directors. Even at best, in dealings with his board, a conductor's tact and diplomacy are often tried to their utmost. And Bernstein was planning a series of sweeping innovations which would break radically with Philharmonic tradition. It would not be sufficient for the board merely to "go along" and refrain from dragging its feet. If his first season was to be a success, the board must believe in his ideas and give them wholehearted support.

Would the board back him up? Or would they consider him merely a brash young upstart, rushing into innovation for innovation's sake?

A strongly marked Bernstein trait is his capacity for making and keeping friends. It was to a friend of long standing that he voiced his misgivings about the Philharmonic.

The friend understood perfectly; understood, too, that the Philharmonic would not get full value from its new conductor if he were otherwise than calm, relaxed, and confident at his first board meeting.

A quiet word was dropped here and there in the proper places. Exactly how this was managed is nobody's business but the Philharmonic's; but at the first meeting, the board rose in standing tribute to its young new Musical Director.

After so charming a gesture, restraint would

have been impossible on either side. Bernstein was his usual buoyant, sparkling self as he outlined plans for his first Philharmonic season. The board for its part had the agreeable sensation that a fresh breeze was blowing through the board room.

The Philharmonic season, Bernstein explained, instead of being a hodgepodge made up of whatever works a given conductor felt like conducting at any given moment, was to be an integrated whole, planned around a central unifying theme. As a start, Bernstein proposed "The American Composer," past, present, and future.

The formal Thursday evening concerts were to be replaced by informal "previews." Here the conductor could chat informally with his audience and clarify the significance of the music. The tested formula which had made Bernstein an outstanding TV personality was now to be placed at the service of the Philharmonic.

The board was fascinated. So, later on, were the Philharmonic subscribers. Some guest conductors were frankly perplexed as to what to do on Thursday evenings. Not all spoke English well, and few shared Bernstein's expository gifts.

By and large, however, the Philharmonic in Bernstein's first season was off to a flying start. All doubt was removed when the box office returns began to come in. Business was picking up.

With the orchestra itself, Bernstein moved cautiously, but firmly, and in the right direction. As Musical Director of the Philharmonic, it no longer sufficed for him to be "strictly one of the boys." Somehow the always-vexing problem of orchestral discipline had to be solved. Bernstein was astute enough to see that he could not solve it by means of Toscaninian invective. For one thing, he confesses, he is not very good at that branch of conducting. "It's not in my nature," he says.

Also, too many of the players remembered Toscanini. Too many of them, for that matter, remembered Bernstein's own debut. With most of them, he had been on a first-name basis for fifteen years as "Lenny." To call him anything else would have been affectation. Bernstein was still paying the penalty of being the boy wonder who had made good.

A Philharmonic player recalls how tactfully Bernstein clarified his new status with the orchestra. Once he had completed a series of concerts and guest conductors were about to take over, Bernstein thanked the players for their co-operation, which he told them had made their concerts a success. Then he said:

"I always used to laugh at Koussevitzky because he hated having guest conductors. Now I have to go away and I feel just the way Koussy did. I don't want a lot of strangers coming in and messing up my orchestra."

The Philharmonic men were greatly tickled by this confidence. All the same, a line had been drawn, a point quietly but unmistakably made. If it was Lenny's orchestra, then by the same token Lenny was Head Man. Authority had been asserted, and not challenged.

Bernstein himself recalls that after he had become musical director, "the first rehearsal was a kind of test."

On that occasion, they were rehearsing Mendelssohn's familiar "Italian" Symphony, which any first-class orchestra could perform in its sleep. Bernstein began taking the symphony apart as if it were a difficult score being played for the first time. He spent two hours on the first movement alone, going over the music bar by bar.

"I could tell from their faces," Bernstein recalls, "they were thinking, 'Is this what it's going to be like under Bernstein? He's treating us like children.' At the end of the two hours, I said, 'Now let's run through the whole thing.' When they had finished, the men stood up and applauded. They could tell themselves, 'We're good.' And they were."

Chapter 17

DURING THE BUSY YEARS which led up to his Philharmonic engagement, Bernstein, somehow, was still finding time to compose.

A major work commissioned by the Koussevitzky Foundation was *Serenade*, for violin, strings, and percussion.

The most interesting thing which can be written about a musical work is the composer's opinion of it. The day after he finished the score, Bernstein wrote this description of *Serenade*:

There is no literal program for this "Serenade," despite the fact that it resulted from a re-reading of Plato's charming dialogue, "The Symposium." The music, like the dialogue, is a series of related statements in praise of love, and generally follows the Platonic form through the succession of speakers at the banquet. The "relatedness" of the movements does not depend on common thematic material, but rather on a system whereby each movement evolves out of elements in the preceding one.

For the benefit of those interested in literary allusion, I might suggest the following points as guideposts:

I. Phaedrus; Pausanius (Lento, Allegro). Phaedrus opens the symposium with a lyrical strain in praise of Eros, the god of love. (Fugato, begun by the solo violin). Pausanius continues by describing the duality of lover and beloved. This is expressed in a classical sonata-allegro, based on the material of the opening fugato.

II. Aristophanes (Allegretto). Aristophanes does not play the role of clown in this dialogue, but instead that of the bedtime story-teller, invoking the fairytale mythology of love.

III. Eruxymathus (Presto). The physician speaks of bodily harmony as a scientific model for the working of love-patterns. This is an extremely short fugato scherzo, born of a blend of mystery and humor.

IV. Agathon (Adagio). Perhaps the most moving speech of the dialogue, Agathon's panegyric embraces all aspects of love's powers, charms and functions. This movement is a simple three-part song.

V. Socrates; Alcibiades (Molto tenuto; Allegro molto vivace). Socrates describes his visit to the seer Diotima, quoting her speech on the demonology of love. This is a slow introduction of greater weight than any of the preceding movements; and serves as a highly developed reprise of the middle section of the Agathon movement, thus suggesting a hidden sonata-form. The famous interruption by Alcibiades and his band of drunken revelers ushers in the Allegro, which is an extended Rondo ranging in spirit from agitation through jig-like dance music to joyful celebration. If there is a hint of jazz in the celebration, I hope it will not be taken as anachronistic Greek party-music, but rather the natural expression of a contemporary American composer imbued with the spirit of that timeless dinner-party.

On this latter point, Bernstein appears to be safe, since nobody knows for certain what ancient Greek party-music sounded like. And the anachronism, if such it is, of setting the *Symposium* in the musical idiom of the twentieth century seems no more anachronistic than, say, Gluck's in setting *Alcestis* in the idiom of the eighteenth.

Nothing in Bernstein's career has given him more satisfaction than *Serenade*. He considers it his best score. It is a large-scale work, a big design brought to a successful conclusion. The composition with which it most invites comparison is *The Age of Anxiety*. In *Serenade,* however, the composer is more assured, more at his ease, with greater mastery over what Schumann called "the stubborn materials of his craft." Experience has given the composer a surer hand and clearer vision.

Particularly impressive is the songlike Adagio, which gives the solo violinist ample opportunity to show how eloquently he can perform. As a matter of fact, the solo part is fluently and idiomatically written for the instrument all through. In its unity, coherence, and musical logic, *Serenade* shows its composer arrived on a new, higher plateau of artistic development.

194

Serenade had its first performance at the Venice Festival on September 12, 1954. Bernstein conducted and Isaac Stern was the soloist. The following spring, Stern played the work with Munch and the B. S. O. in Boston, and with Bernstein and the Symphony of the Air in New York.

Another venture into the theater was the writing of incidental music for *The Lark,* a Jean Anouilh play starring Julie Harris which opened in November, 1955.

And a brilliant display of Bernstein's virtuosity as a jazzman had been *Prelude, Fugue and Riffs,* an orchestral work which had its first performance under the composer's direction on the *Omnibus* telecast of October 16, 1955.

A year later, on October 7, 1956, Bernstein on *Omnibus* discussed the evolution of the American musical, starting with *The Black Crook* of 1855. It was, said Bernstein, a unique and peculiarly American institution, falling midway between the two opposed poles of opera and variety show.

At that time, Bernstein was much preoccupied with musicals. He had just finished writing one.

As early as 1951, it had been trade gossip that Bernstein and playwright Lillian Hellman were planning to collaborate on a theater work. For one reason and another, the project had been shelved. Finally, in 1954, the two were able to start their

195

joint project, that of turning Voltaire's *Candide* into a musical satire.

Bernstein was enchanted with the idea. He had treasured *Candide,* that touchstone of humor and wisdom, since his student days. Setting it to music would be a labor of love.

The Bernstein-Hellman team was reinforced by the combined talents of Dorothy Parker, Richard Wilbur, and the late John La Touche, who were to write the lyrics. With so many first-rate creative brains at work, and a universally loved masterpiece as the starting point, it seemed that *Candide* could not miss.

And yet the musical, begun with such high hopes, bogged down.

"Looking back on it," Richard Wilbur says, "I can see that everyone fell down. There was no single villain. Lillian Hellman doesn't really like musicals. Lenny's music got more and more pretentious and smashy—the audience forgot what was happening to the characters. Lillian's book got to be mere connective tissue. And I was inclined to be too literary and stubborn."

As rehearsals progressed, Bernstein, more knowledgeable than his colleagues, had a premonition of disaster. This was shown, in somewhat roundabout fashion, by a piece which he wrote for the Sunday *Times* of November 16, 1956. With typical Bernsteinian classicism it took the form of a dialogue, between Leonard Bernstein and his Id. The latter appeared as Bernstein was considering "one of the knottiest problems of the score, namely: Does this F-sharp sound as if it belonged in a Broadway musical?

Id (sneering). Broadway musical! I can but smile. Why do you concern yourself with that pitiful F-sharp? Your problem began long before this, over a month ago, on television. Have you forgotten that in front of millions of Americans viewing *Omnibus* on October 7 you committed yourself forever to a definition of American musical comedy as being what it is largely because of the American elements in it? Your only problem is that you have betrayed your own definition. Now let's have that F-sharp.

L. B. Wait. As always, you attack me at my weakest moment. But let's be fair. I never actually defined American musical comedy. I was only trying to describe it and to provoke thought about it by throwing out leading ideas.

Id. Of course, you said all that, but only after ninety minutes of examples and discussions designed to show that the whole development of musical comedy in this country is based on its ever-increasing alliance with American elements, American subject-matter, American themes and the American musical vernacular, by which it turns out you meant jazz. And then you went on with a whole other catalogue of Americanisms; our tempo, our way of moving, our moral attitudes, our timing, our kind of humor and all the rest. You certainly don't deny that?

L. B. I certainly don't. It's true. I believe it.

Id. Well, then, poor fellow, how come that you, of all people, are sitting in this hotel writing an American musical comedy based on Voltaire's *Candide*, that great American classic?

L. B. Voltaire's satire is international. It throws light on all the dark places, whether American or European. Of course, it's not an American book, but the matters with which it is concerned are as valid for us as for any —and sometimes I think they are especially valid for us in America. And they are also the charges made by Voltaire against his own society.

Id. I see. I also see that what you're talking about isn't a musical comedy at all—at least not in the sense of what you described on the *Omnibus* program. *Candide* is beginning to look to me like a real fine old-fashioned operetta. Or a comic opera, or opera-comique, or whatever that *Omnibus* list of yours was. But not a musical comedy, surely?

L. B. My dear Id, who ever said it wasn't an operetta? If that's all you've been worrying about, then our argument is concluded. You remember I said that one of the most obvious attributes of the operetta is the exotic (to Americans) atmosphere in which it exists, and that the music of the operetta is more serious in musical intent, more highly developed, less like Tin Pan Alley—gay though it may be? I guess *Candide* follows in this tradition, rather than in the pure musical comedy tradition of *Guys and Dolls* or *Wonderful Town*. And now, demon, I hereby exorcise you, and command you to lie down again in peace. Good night.

Id (who always has the last word). Good night. And now, what are you going to do about that F-sharp?

198

It does not require very prescient reading between the lines here to discern a creative artist concerned over a creation which has turned out to be a problem child. It seems clear that Bernstein did not quite know what to make of *Candide*.

Neither, it seemed, did Broadway audiences. *Candide* opened at the Martin Beck Theater on December 12, 1956, and closed seventy-three performances later. For the first time in his career, Bernstein knew what it was to be the composer of a Broadway flop.

Did the failure prove *Candide* to be without merit? Certainly Bernstein had lavished on the score the utmost resources of his musical imagination. The overture, a bubbling-over piece in the great opera buffa tradition, has shown sufficient vitality to stand on its own as a concert piece, and has been played at numerous orchestral concerts.

The musically rich score also included melodies both wistful and merry, parodies of operatic arias, music hall ballads, folk songs, trios, quartets, choral numbers, and such dance forms as the waltz, mazurka, gavotte, and tango. Musically, Bernstein had outdone himself; no previous musical by him was quite comparable to the *Candide* score.

One thing was certain about *Candide*—people felt strongly about it, one way or the other. Those who liked it felt a contemporary masterpiece had been undeservedly snubbed by the Broadway public. Some of them felt its title may have frightened away those who did not know the work and supposed Voltaire's *Candide* to be much like Racine's *Phèdre*. With a different, more commercial title, they maintained, the musical might have had a longer run.

Brooks Atkinson made the point that "the eighteenth-century philosophical tale is not ideal material for a theatre show." Philosophy seldom is. Much fun has been made of Italian opera for its preoccupation with love, hatred, jealousy, and revenge. But these are universal human passions, felt and understood by audiences everywhere. The creator of a successful opera or operetta is a showman, working swiftly in bright colors with broad, bold strokes. Over-refined subtleties do not always come off in performance.

Beaumarchais's ironic rule of thumb for a libretto was, "What is too silly to be spoken can be sung." Perhaps the corollary is that what is too serious to sing about should be spoken. If one accepts the Atkinson thesis that *Candide* is inherently non-theatrical, then the failure cannot be ascribed to Bernstein's score; neither Bernstein nor any other composer could have brought it off.

But *Candide,* although a failure on Broadway, stubbornly refused to die. A concert version toured the United States. And when the musical opened in London in April, 1959, British playgoers hailed it with delight. It is quite possible that Broadway playgoers may have another look at *Candide,* and may revise their opinion.

Whatever disappointment Bernstein may have experienced was only temporary. He was already at work on another musical, whose immediate and lasting success would more than make amends for *Candide.*

Chapter 18

I N T H E T I M E - H O N O R E D M A N N E R of things theatrical, *West Side Story* was originally titled *East Side Story*. (In a moment of aberration, it was also briefly known as *Gang Way!*)

As originally conceived by Jerome Robbins, the work was to have been a musical version of *Romeo and Juliet*, set on the Lower East Side of Manhattan and dealing with the love of a boy and girl of different races and religious faiths, caught up in the enmity of rival street gangs.

The idea was kicked around, often unmercifully, by his collaborators—writer Arthur Laurents and Bernstein.

All were drawn to the idea. It had the timeliness and impact of a tabloid headline. As of 1955-56, race tensions in parts of New York City had risen to the pitch of open warfare. New Yorkers were recalling nostalgically the days when one thought nothing of walking through Central Park after sunset.

Race antagonisms of New York adolescents, however, cut across religious lines. White Roman Catholics battled Puerto Ricans of their own faith; white Protestants clashed with Negroes.

One day in 1955, Laurents and Bernstein were turning over these ideas beside the swimming pool of the Beverly Hills Hotel.

"We realized the religious issue had become extraneous," Laurents recalls. "Juvenile delinquency had become the problem. We thought in terms of the Mexicans in Los Angeles. Then it was just a step to the Puerto Ricans in New York."

It was like finding the key to a puzzle. Once found, everything fitted neatly into place. The collaborators set to work, achieving such quick results that producers Griffith and Prince were able to send out a casting call early in 1956.

Then began what Jerome Robbins would call, in retrospect, the most difficult of his ten casting assignments since *On the Town*.

"No stars," the call read. Since it was a play about adolescents, the players had to look believably young. That ruled out established theater names.

But not just any young actors would do. They

also had to be dependable performers, with the professionalism which comes only with experience. They had to be real singers, since Bernstein's music called for more than mere declamation. A further complication was that Bernstein and Robbins wanted dancers who could also double as a chorus of vocalists.

This was asking a lot, Robbins discovered when he began his talent hunt. Doggedly he explored all known habitats of singers who could act and dancers who could sing. He went to settlement music schools, college *a cappela* choirs, night clubs, operatic choruses, and the card files of radio-TV and theatrical agents. Among America's millions surely enough young people could be found to play the thirty-eight roles in *West Side Story*.

The search lasted eight months, and took Robbins to California and back. At times, it looked hopeless. The collaborators wondered whether they ought not to lower their sights, to settle for less than they had originally hoped for. But always the final vote was, "No compromise." The show could go over to another season instead.

And that was what eventually happened. Not until September 26, 1957, was *West Side Story* to open.

Its first-night performance at the Winter Garden proved the wisdom of delay. *West Side Story* had been worth waiting for. Not in a long time had the Broadway theater had flung in its face so violent an explosion of drama. It was more than an updating of *Romeo and Juliet*. Shakespeare's people spoke musical blank verse and held to the chivalric code of honor. The players in *West Side Story* communicated in vulgar guttersnipe language. Their chivalry was the gunman's code of daring and loyalty to the mob. They mirrored with frightening clarity the ugliness and raw violence swirling beneath the surface of a great city.

The balcony scene, which took place on the fire escape of a Puerto Rican tenement, though lacking the magic of Shakespeare's verses, was all the more poignant for the squalor of its surroundings. The hopeless love of the boy and girl, the first fine and true emotion felt by either of them, was even more touching in its contrast to the brutality and hatred all around them.

To this shocker of raw violence, Bernstein added music which was in many respects the most remarkable he had yet composed. Not that *West Side Story* is a pretty score. It is a far cry from George M. Cohan's merry bugle calls, or the sweet, singable tunes of Victor Herbert and Jerome Kern.

What Bernstein did was to employ the musical and orchestral resources available to a highly sophisticated musician to create a score bursting with vitality and dramatic tension. His music powerfully underscored the stage situation. It gave an impression of nervous drive, hostility, callousness, distrust. Musically, it was welded to the drama as firmly as were Jerome Robbins' grim, joyless, sinister dance numbers in choreographic terms. It is not often that separate theater elements are so thoroughly fused. *West Side Story* had impact. Some playgoers were overwhelmed; others recoiled in horror from its grimly realistic portrayal of city life; very few were unmoved.

From the start, it was clear that *West Side Story* would make amends for *Candide*. Advance ticket sales guaranteed the musical a solid run. With *West Side Story* under control, Bernstein was characteristically off at once. Before the week was out, he was in Tel Aviv for the opening of the Fredric R. Mann Auditorium.

The auditorium project, one dear to Bernstein's heart, had had its inception during the 1951 U.S. tour of the Israel Philharmonic. At a reception in Philadelphia, members of the orchestra had met Mann, who was shocked to learn that the Israel Philharmonic had no proper concert hall. For fifteen years, it had been barnstorming about the country, playing in movie theaters, playhouses, club rooms, and other makeshift locations. An auditorium was a luxury which could be postponed; the new nation had other things which more urgently needed doing.

Mann disagreed. He told the visiting musicians

they should, and could, and before long would, have a concert hall worthy of the orchestra.

That this was not just cocktail party conversation was shown when the energetic Philadelphian swung into action. As a start, Mann contributed $250,000 and raised $150,000 more. The Mann Auditorium as finally completed in the summer of 1957 was a $2,000,000 air-conditioned hall seating 2,700 listeners, with standing room for three hundred more. Inside its marble and glass facade was a fan-shaped auditorium, spreading upward from the stage, with a ceiling suspended from a copper-domed roof.

A notable audience, including Mann and other visitors from the United States, filled every seat on October 2, 1957, when Bernstein led the Israel Philharmonic in a "Festival Prelude" written for the occasion by Israeli composer Noam Sheriff. Soloists for the concert were pianist Artur Rubinstein, violinist Isaac Stern and cellist Paul Tortelier.

The enthusiasm created by the new hall, the distinguished soloists, and Israel's favorite conductor can be imagined. After years of wandering, the Israel Philharmonic had found a home.

From Tel Aviv, Bernstein set out to re-travel familiar territory. He was under the constant scrutiny of movie cameras; a filmed report of his tour of Israel was to be shown on the *Omnibus* telecast of December 1.

Then it was time to scramble back to New York,

where he was to begin his first season as joint conductor with Mitropoulos of the Philharmonic.

Concertgoers noted with interest that Bernstein was now using a baton. Heretofore, the expressive use of hands alone had been as integral a part of his performance as of Stokowski's.

Bernstein explained that, having wrenched his back during the tour of Israel, he had taken to the stick as a way of getting a more precise beat with less effort. The stick, he predicted, would "add five years to my life."

He found, however, that the baton took getting used to. It had a disconcerting way of slipping from his grasp at impassioned moments in the music, causing Philharmonic players to duck apprehensively as it whirled past.

Helpfully, Adolph Green suggested that Bernstein tie a string to the baton and loop the string about his wrist.

Bernstein glowered and explained that that sort of thing was not done.

Chapter 19

THE DC-6's CARRYING members of the Philharmonic, flying past snow-covered peaks 20,000 feet high, touched down at the world's highest commercial airport, at La Paz, Bolivia. It was quite literally the high spot of the tour which in the spring of 1958 presented thirty-nine concerts by the Philharmonic in twelve Latin American countries.

Native Indians crowded around the plane, ready to welcome the visitors in traditional Bolivian fashion.

Immediately, a loudspeaker began to crackle. Please! No welcoming shots were to be fired!

Philharmonic players who understood Spanish looked at each other in astonishment. What was going on?

It turned out that a revolution was imminent, and gunfire at the airport might have been mistaken for a sign that action had begun there.

Bernstein and the orchestra found that La Paz's 12,500-foot altitude took getting used to. In the rarefied air, the slightest exertion set them panting.

Local authorities fortunately had anticipated this and had set out portable oxygen flasks for the visitors. A restorative whiff between numbers aided conductor and orchestra in performing with their usual flair.

It had been predicted that the Philharmonic woodwinds could not summon up enough breath control to get through a concert at La Paz. The woodwinds managed ably, however, by fitting their instruments with thin, "weak" reeds which would vibrate at the slightest breath pressure. When the Philharmonic again reached sea level its woodwinds were a good half-tone flat.

The South American tour was an experience not soon forgotten, even by so widely traveled an orchestra as the Philharmonic. The men were fascinated by the spectacular, infinitely varied scenery, with its many pictorial possibilities (Philharmonic players are photographers almost to a man). They marveled at the sudden sharp contrasts between the modern, up-to-date seaboard cities and the primitive villages of the interior, seeming much as they must have looked when the first Europeans came.

Above all, they marveled at the furore stirred up everywhere by their arrival. No town was too small to hang across its main street a "Bienvenida Filarmonica" banner and supply a cheering crowd at the airport.

The Philharmonic found audiences cordial and knowledgeable. The Latin American nations have a long tradition of music-making. *Il Guarany*, by the Brazilian Antonio Carlos Gomes, was the first successful opera to be written by a composer of the Western Hemisphere. As a cadet aboard the Russian warship *Almaz*, Rimsky-Korsakov found Rio de Janeiro a music-loving city in 1863; the Philharmonic found it so in 1958.

Few orchestras south of the Rio Grande, however, can match the playing of ours. Nor, for that matter, can any but a few of the finest European groups. Orchestral playing, in this country in the present century, has attained a pitch of excellence seldom matched elsewhere. One cause has been the unique fusion and blending of French, German, and Italian traditions of orchestral playing and the resultant tendency to adopt the best features of each. In the larger cities, orchestras have had reasonably adequate budgets and have been able to offer salaries to tempt the world's finest conducting talents. There been an adequate supply of capable musicians, with splendid conservatories constantly turning out replacements. Finally and perhaps most importantly, there has been an interested and appreciative public.

All these things make the sound of a major American orchestra unique and, to those who have not heard it before, a revelation.

Latin America had not heard this sound in a good while—since 1940, in fact. That was the year when Toscanini made his South American tour with the NBC Symphony Orchestra, and Stokowski, to the intense annoyance of Toscanini and NBC, also went there with his All-American Youth Orchestra.

Latin Americans told Bernstein the hiatus had been much too long.

With Bernstein and Mitropoulos alternating as conductors, the Philharmonic played in all sorts of places. It performed in beautifully decorated nineteenth-century municipal opera houses, and atop an improvised stage on the shore of Lake Maracaibo. In Caracas, it drew a record-breaking crowd to the Concha Acoustica, which Bernstein pronounced the finest outdoor theater in which he had ever performed.

In Rio de Janeiro, Mitropoulos led the orchestra before a capacity audience at the Municipal Theater in a televised concert featuring works of the Brazilian composer Camargo Guarnieri. Two days later, Bernstein conducted a concert which drew 15,000 listeners to Rio's Maracanazinha Basketball Stadium.

In Chile, leaving the orchestra to his colleague,

Bernstein slipped away with his wife for a brief skiing vacation in the Chilean Andes.

At Quito, Ecuador, Bernstein encountered a countryman who was there on the same good will business as himself—Vice-President Richard M. Nixon.

Some observers could not help commenting that in the department of good will, Bernstein and the Philharmonic were getting rather the best of it.

Perhaps this was rather unfair to Nixon. News photographs left no doubt that the attack on his car in Caracas was not a spontaneous public outburst but a carefully planned "incident," carried out by a small but well organized group while Venezuelan police unaccountably looked the other way.

But the Philharmonic appeared time after time in politically tense situations, where possibilities for trouble were great, and received the warmest of welcomes.

The orchestra reached Bogota on election day. Despite the political ferment and an abortive police revolt, the Philharmonic concert was well attended and enthusiastically cheered.

At Caracas, the concert took place on May Day, the traditional time for political demonstrations. All business in the city came to a halt; but the open-air concert took place as scheduled. The amphitheater's 7,000 seats were filled and other thousands were turned away. Scalpers were buying tickets at a premium of three hundred per cent and reselling them at four hundred. Latin Americans paid Bernstein and the Philharmonic their supreme compliment; it was, they said, like a bull-fight.

Bernstein felt that the very nature of the Philharmonic tour gave it something of an advantage over the Vice-Presidential party. The Philharmonic, he pointed out, "came only to speak music, to do delightful things. The other mission came to present a new policy for the future. We had a mission for all time—Haydn, Gershwin, and so on."

The Philharmonic and the "other mission" met at Quito, Ecuador. The Vice-President greeted Bernstein affably and invited him to hold a joint press conference. Nixon confessed that he was "a poorer piano player than Harry Truman" and could not play the violin at all.

The tour continued in an unbroken string of triumphs. In Buenos Aires, the orchestra received such an ovation it was obliged to play an encore, although this was unheard-of and contrary to Teatro Colón policy.

Of the concert in Rio de Janeiro, a critic wrote: "Since we were visited by the NBC Symphony with Toscanini many years ago, it was the most beauti-

214

ful symphonic night we have had at the Municipal Theater."

For a Montevideo reviewer, the orchestra "forms one prodigious instrument in the hands of its imaginative conductor." And a Santiago critic found "a perfection in detail, outstanding quality and disciplined control such as have never been disclosed to the Chilean public in the past."

It was in Santiago that Bernstein received a touch of personal adulation straight out of the nineteenth century: applauding crowds followed him through the streets before and after the concerts.

If Latin America idolized Bernstein, it was not without cause. Aside from the glamour of his position, Bernstein had made himself a most gracious guest. Since his marriage, his household had been bilingual, speaking both English and Spanish. Now he drew on this resource to greet his audiences.

We say of a man that he "speaks our language." So does Latin America. Bernstein was *muy simpatico.*

Then there were the national anthems—dozens of them, it sometimes appeared—to which Bernstein gave the same meticulous attention as to other works on the program. Each concert began with "The Star-Spangled Banner" and the local anthem. This may seem an unimportant detail until it is realized that some audiences had never heard their anthem performed by a group remotely approaching the power and sonority of the New York Philharmonic. The impact on listeners was immense. At Caracas, the President of Venezuela came backstage at intermission to request Bernstein to repeat the national anthem at the end of the concert.

The tour came to an end in Mexico City, where Bernstein led the orchestra in Carlos Chavez's *Sinfonia India*. The composer was in the audience. Bernstein summoned him to the stage, where Chavez embraced his American colleague, to the huge delight of a cheering audience.

Next day, the Philharmonic played the last of its thirty-nine Latin American concerts before an audience of 13,000 in Mexico City's National Auditorium.

An official City Hall welcome awaited Bernstein, Mitropoulos, and the orchestra upon their return. Each member of the orchestra received from City Council President Abe Stark an illuminated scroll commemorating the orchestra's services to music and to international good will. The formal ceremony was almost disrupted when Bernstein, borrowing the bandmaster's stick, led the Department of Sanitation Band in Sousa's "Stars and Stripes Forever."

After this pleasant accolade, it was time to get back to business. In just one week, Bernstein was to lead the concert opening the forty-first season of summer concerts at Lewisohn Stadium. As usual, he had no time to spare.

Chapter 20

SEPTEMBER 26, 1958, was a richly satisfying day for Bernstein. On that date, *West Side Story* had been running for a year and showed every sign of continuing for another. And the forthcoming Thursday "preview" concerts had rung up the largest pre-season ticket sale in the history of the New York Philharmonic.

Bernstein had caused a stir with his promise that at the previews informality would be carried to the point of musicians' appearing in ordinary street clothes. So great had been the agitation that on second thought Bernstein decided it would be better to shock the subscribers by degrees. At the opening concert, on October 2, both he and the orchestra wore their customary evening dress.

Early the following week, Philharmonic men were digging into packing boxes and going goggle-eyed at what they found. The "preview" uniforms had arrived. They were black tunics with stiff cadet collars, closely resembling the alpaca rehearsal jackets worn by Toscanini, Bruno Walter, and other conductors of the older generation. Bernstein's was the same as the musicians' except for the sporty touch of a breast-pocket white handkerchief.

"Toscanini is back," said Philharmonic players who remembered the old days. Others assured colleagues they looked like bellhops at the Astor.

Bernstein arrived, beaming, to help model. The jackets were his idea. He felt they symbolized the combination of concert-hall formality and unpredictability of the previews. Besides, he pointed out, the jackets were comfortable to play and conduct in.

The new Philharmonic jackets made their appearance at the season's second preview, on October 9. Whether or not they tickled the audience is difficult to say; the concert began with unexpected solemnity. Pope Pius XII had just died, and Bernstein asked his audience to stand with him in tribute to "the passing of a very great man." Guffaws, under such circumstances, were unthinkable.

Another tribute was paid in November, when Rodzinski died. Bernstein had undergone a certain amount of hazing from this bearish master; yet it had been through Rodzinski that he had had his first big opportunity. And by walking out on the Philharmonic, Rodzinski had in a sense prepared the way for Bernstein's own appointment.

Bernstein announced that he was dedicating the November 28 concert to Rodzinski's memory. He recalled, with the self-effacing modesty which is one of his most disarming traits, the debt of gratitude which he owed to the older musician. "But more than that," Bernstein added, "I would like to pay tribute to Mr. Rodzinski because he was a great conductor."

It is at such moments that even Bernstein's bitterest detractors are obliged to concede that he has an appealing side.

Bernstein had jokingly predicted that his first Philharmonic season would be "like putting together a jigsaw puzzle." He soon saw how right he was. More than once, he regretted having undertaken to do a survey of American music within the rigid framework of an orchestral season. It was too late, however; he was already committed.

And if there were problems, there were rewards as well. One came when Bernstein was able to surprise his audience by bringing on stage Wallingford Riegger, seventy-two; John Becker, seventy-three; and Carl Ruggles, eighty-two.

"My dear friends," said Bernstein, in one of his carefully prepared speeches which managed to sound chatty and unrehearsed, "we are having the rare privilege and honor of hearing the music of three grand old men. They were sweet enough to come on stage so you could meet them."

Audience reaction showed listeners, too, felt it a rare privilege and honor.

"Isn't it wonderful to be able to have three original, authentic pioneers with us?" Bernstein continued. "It is because music in America started so late that pioneers are still living. They are the real article, salty, peppery, crusty, unconventional, and eternally young in spirit. They all have one quality that is truly American — breaking new ground, clearing out old weeds, seeking out new frontiers."

Bernstein's enthusiasm, as usual, communicated itself to the audience. This was not the language of a conductor paying mere lip-service to the cause of American music. For that matter, not all conductors would have scheduled on one program the music of three such individualists as Becker, Ruggles, and Riegger.

The Riegger work, *Music for Orchestra*, Op. 50, is based on a "tone-row." This, Bernstein explained to his hearers, in its simplest form consisted of the twelve notes of the chromatic scale, played in predetermined order with no note being repeated, then in reverse order, and finally inverted. In literary terms, it would be somewhat like using

221

the twenty-six letters of the alphabet without repeating one letter, then going through the list in reverse order, and finally turning the letters upside down. By imagining what it would be like even to leave a note for the milkman using this method, one can appreciate the severity of the intellectual discipline which the tone-row imposes upon musicians. Arnold Schoenberg, its originator, said of the tone-row that "little has been added, and much has been taken away" from the composer's vocabulary.

Bernstein's explanation of the Riegger piece, some observers noted, lasted nine minutes; the duration of the work itself was eight. For Bernstein, the obvious rejoinder was that if conductors felt it necessary to spend years on a Brahms symphony, nine minutes were little enough for a work in a difficult and unfamiliar idiom.

His initial stint with the Philharmonic finished, Bernstein was off to Paris to conduct the Lamoureux and French National Orchestras, and to Milan for a guest engagement at La Scala. He returned to New York at the end of November, just in time to speak at the annual Friends of the Philharmonic luncheon at the Waldorf-Astoria.

What Bernstein had to say electrified the luncheon: "I will not conduct any other orchestra in the world while I am musical director of the New York Philharmonic." The reason, he said, was that he obtained "the fullest possible satisfaction from conducting this, the most beautiful and flexible of all orchestras."

There was another reason, but one which Bernstein was not eager to publicize. For the first time in his career, he felt tired.

"I can't understand it," he confessed to a friend in some perplexity. "Everything used to be so easy."

Now he was discovering that at forty, one has not the resilience of twenty-three.

And the scope of his activity was, if anything, wider than ever. To the always punishing Philharmonic schedule had been added virtually a supplementary season, the result of the Philharmonic telecasts.

Youthful admiration for Bernstein had led to the formation from coast to coast of TV listening clubs, whose members watched the Philharmonic telecasts and discussed them. Bernstein and the Philharmonic had unearthed a whole new teen-age listening audience. This was a situation which orchestra and conductor were eager to exploit to the full; a symphony orchestra can never catch its subscribers too young.

The Carnegie Hall rehearsals of the Philharmonic, which heretofore had been almost as closely guarded as the Eleusinian mysteries, at Bernstein's suggestion were opened to the public. High school youngsters swarmed in by bus and subway to see how a great symphony orchestra is whipped into shape, and to gaze worshipfully at its conductor.

After a solid afternoon of Beethoven, youngsters rushed to the stage for autographs and a word with their idol. One bright-eyed, pony-tailed teenager summed up Bernstein: "He's the furriest."

At a certain age, admiration can take no higher form.

The Philharmonic telecasts did gratifying things to the incomes of Philharmonic players. But the initial season made it clear that life with Bernstein would be strenuous.

A typical TV Saturday for Bernstein began at the pre-dawn hour of 5:30 A.M., when he walked the short block from his apartment to the stage door of Carnegie Hall. On the stage, a CBS television crew had been at work since midnight. The hall had been in use until eleven o'clock the previous night, and setting up the complex TV equipment required six hours.

Bernstein had been asked to report at 6:00 A.M. for preliminary run-throughs with cameramen and sound engineers. At 7:00, there was a rehearsal with a chorus of boys and girls from the High School of Music and Art, who were performing Aaron Copland's opera for young people, *The Second Hurricane*. Bernstein had had his first rehearsal with the youthful choristers three days before. The performance was set for noon. It would be recorded on film and telecast over the CBS network the following day.

At eight o'clock, sleepy members of the Philharmonic were on stage, ready for a run-through of the opera with orchestra. *The Second Hurricane* received its final polishing, with nervous tension building up on all sides as the hands of the stage clock went round and round toward noon.

At a quarter to ten, Bernstein and CBS technicians met in a small backstage office. The consensus was that the performance was terrible. The youthful principals were missing cues, forgetting lines. Voices did not balance properly. Bernstein had two hours in which to pull the show together.

Bernstein finished his cigarette and went back for the dress rehearsal. This time, he entered to applause. The hall was filling up with patrons of the Philharmonic's Young People's Series. Another run-through of the Copland work followed. This time it was punctuated at appropriate spots by cheers and laughter. The audience relished being part of a TV show.

At 11:30, Bernstein went to his dressing room to be made up for the performance. The formal concert began at four minutes past noon. The young performers were alert, on their toes. By some subtle alchemy of the conductor-performer relationship, the hour-long opera was polished and well paced. Principals came in smartly on cues which they had muffed in rehearsal. Choristers sang like professionals. The audience loved it.

The Philharmonic men scattered, leaving Bernstein surrounded by autograph hunters of all ages. Then he was summoned back to the vacant stage. Someone had fouled up his closing remarks, which would have to be re-recorded. A make-up artist hastily applied powder to his cheeks, now smudged with lipstick. Then, taking a deep breath, Bernstein mounted the podium to address the non-existent audience for the benefit of the TV cameras.

"Since this is the last concert of the season, I want to take this opportunity to thank you. . . ." The stint finished, Bernstein sagged. "I am so tired," he said, "I can't talk."

It was 1:45 when Bernstein was finally able to break away, more than eight hours after he had entered the hall, to have lunch with Betty Comden and Adolph Green.

After lunch, Bernstein napped briefly. Then his osteopath came over to work the stiffness out of his back. There was still work to be done. He was to conduct Beethoven's towering *Missa Solemnis* at the evening Philharmonic concert.

The magnificent pages of the Beethoven score acted on Bernstein like a shot of adrenalin. He was too elated for sleep. In order to unwind, he went to hear Lena Horne at the Waldorf-Astoria. When he finally went to bed, it was after two A.M.

Given a succession of such days, it is not surprising that Bernstein sometimes feels tired.

Chapter 21

BERNSTEIN'S LIFE, so long that of a wandering minstrel, now began stabilizing itself around the Philharmonic season.

He has so far kept his promise to conduct no other orchestra while he is musical director of the Philharmonic. During the Philharmonic season, the Bernsteins, their children, and two Chilean women servants spend most of their time in their big apartment on Fifty-seventh Street.

Miss Coates's apartment, which also functions as Bernstein's office, is in the same building. From these two centers and the "thinking room" are co-ordinated Bernstein's incessant activities.

Summer vacations are spent at Martha's Vineyard, and for a weekend retreat there is a small white house on a hill in Connecticut.

The Bernsteins make a handsome couple at theater first nights, and entertain frequently on non-Philharmonic evenings. At a typical party one may meet family, in the person of sister Shirley or brother Burton (now a writer for *The New Yorker*) and his wife; old friends like Betty Comden and Adolph Green; theater personalities such as Lena Horne, Harry Belafonte, or Vivien Leigh.

Bernstein's working schedule nowadays is not what it used to be. Bruno Zirato, who recently retired as managing director of the Philharmonic, used to reproach him with affectionate severity for over-extending himself: "Lenny, you are like a whore—you cannot say no." But Bernstein is learning.

Bernstein's first season with the Philharmonic set the pattern which others have followed. The orchestra's playing season steadily lengthened; TV and recording sessions brought added income; subscriptions flourished as they had hardly done since the days of Toscanini. There were other big, spectacular tours, with box office records shattered in all directions.

At Las Vegas, Nevada, where the only previous orchestral performance on record was a concert by the Utah Symphony, 7,000 listeners turned out to hear the Philharmonic under Bernstein.

For local managers, the Philharmonic offered something new—"Bernstein insurance." Managers who feared receipts would fall off in case of Bernstein's non-appearance might insure against that eventuality at three per cent, or thirty dollars per thousand, of anticipated lost revenue.

Among highlights of the 1959 tour were the orchestra's performances in Moscow. On August 22, Bernstein and the Philharmonic made a hit with their knowledgeable interpretation of the Shostakovitch Fifth Symphony. In addition, Bernstein had astonished the Muscovites by a feat not usual there, that of conducting a Mozart concerto from the piano. Listeners cheered, shouted, clapped in unison and cried: "Bravo! Bis! Encore!"

Linguist Bernstein, from a couple of weeks' intensive study of Russian, was able to reply: *"Bolshoieh spasibo!"* ("Many thanks!")

On his birthday, Bernstein created a sensation by leading Stravinsky's *Sacre du printemps* and Charles Ives's *The Unanswered Question.* The Stravinsky work, he told his audience, "created a musical revolution five years before your revolution. Music has never been the same since that performance. Then, five years after your revolution, he created another revolution by turning to neoclassic form."

For this somewhat complex idea, Bernstein felt obliged to rely on an interpreter. Here the language barrier proved a handicap. The interpreter distorted Bernstein's thought by using the word *skandal,* which means not revolution, but the sort of concert-hall tempest in a teapot induced by the playing of a new work in a puzzling idiom. That was not what Bernstein meant at all; he felt *Le Sacre* to have been a revolution, nothing less.

Bernstein also repeated what he had heard from musicians in Moscow, that the Stravinsky work had not been heard in the Soviet Union in thirty years. From the box of the Soviet Minister of Culture —Philharmonic officials still are not sure whether it was the Minister himself speaking—came an indignant denial: *"Nyet pravda!"*

It turned out that the work had been done in Tallin, Estonia, and excerpts had also been performed as a ballet.

The magazine *Sovyetskaya Kultura* took Bernstein to task over these matters, and also for "insisting" on a repetition of the Ives piece. Eyewitnesses say the insisting was done by the audience, not by Bernstein.

Bernstein had preceded *The Unanswered Question* with an explanation of the piece, and of Ives's music in general, which had aroused the curiosity of listeners. When the music was played, there was such a roar of applause that Bernstein was dumfounded.

In the wings, where a Philharmonic aide was literally jumping up and down with excitement, Bernstein asked, "My God, do you suppose they want an encore?"

"I'd say yes, yes, yes."

Bernstein returned to the stage and held up his hand for silence. "Does this mean you want to hear the music again?"

The answering roar of applause left no doubt.

This was how Bernstein "insisted" on the encore. An interesting sequel was that, in other cities in Russia where Bernstein simply played the work without comment, listeners did not know what to expect and there was no such enthusiasm for Ives as that displayed in Moscow.

The Moscow concert was a huge success, reaching its climax when the librarian of the Moscow Symphony presented Bernstein with an old photograph of Koussevitzky's teacher, Arthur Nikisch. After the concert, Bernstein was greeted cordially by such colleagues as violinist Leonid Kogan, pianist Vladimir Ashkenazy, and composer Aram Khachaturian. (Shostakovitch was out of town, vacationing.)

At the Moscow Conservatory, Bernstein had a charming surprise. Copies of the Clarinet Sonata, his first published work, had found their way to Moscow. Now two student composers had collaborated in writing a set of orchestral variations on a theme from the sonata.

Bernstein looked through the score with lively interest, and delighted the young Soviet musicians by telling them: "Your variations are better than my theme."

One Russian whom Bernstein was especially eager to meet was the late Boris Pasternak. He tried to contact the Nobel Prize author, but without success. A letter addressed to Bernstein in care of the Moscow Conservatory led only to bafflement. It was written in French, and after offering to introduce Bernstein to Pasternak, concluded: "When you go to meet Pasternak, take me along. I want to meet him, too." The signature was indecipherable and there was no return address.

When the Philharmonic returned to Moscow in early September, Bernstein knew Pasternak's address, having obtained it in Leningrad from an artist who knew Pasternak. Two days before the orchestra's final concert, Felicia Bernstein and Steve Rosenfeld, a Russian-speaking member of the Philharmonic staff,* set out to find Pasternak. Bernstein remained at the hotel, writing a TV script.

"We got in a taxi," Rosenfeld says, "and as soon as we were outside Moscow, the driver was lost. We wandered about, asking directions, but nobody knew where this place was. After an hour and a half of this, we were in utter despair. Finally we came out of a pine forest and went through a small village—not a suburb, a real Russian village with

---

* Now of the Washington *Post*.

232

pre-revolutionary carved wooden huts, a muddy road, chickens wandering around, women with *babushkas* around their heads. Suddenly Felicia began screaming. She had turned to say something to me and out of the corner of her eye had seen Pasternak through the rear window of the cab.

"Felicia rushed to Pasternak and began talking, first in French, then in Italian and in Spanish. She was so excited and talked so fast he probably couldn't have understood her in Russian. Then it occurred to us that Pasternak spoke perfectly good English, and we established contact.

"Felicia's clothes were, as always, straight from Bergdorf Goodman. She looked so out of place among the chickens and *babushkas* it was ludicrous. When she dropped her glove, one of the *babushka* ladies picked it up and said, 'Your glove, *Dama'* — 'Milady,' I guess it would be in English. She must have looked to them like a princess out of a fairy tale."

Pasternak invited Rosenfeld and the Bernsteins to dinner that evening. In a pouring rain, they drove up and waited, dripping, while Pasternak and his wife had a lengthy talk in Russian. To the Bernsteins' perplexity and Rosenfeld's quiet amusement, it was a family squabble; the taxi had come to the rear entrance and Mrs. Pasternak did not wish the "honored guests" to enter through her kitchen.

Finally the issue was resolved and an evening of absorbing talk began which did not end until midnight. Pasternak did most of the talking. He described his long search for truth through art, and spoke interestingly about music, in which his tastes were unashamedly old-fashioned. It turned out that he had been eager to meet Bernstein and had written to him, but "they" had intercepted his letter.

At the final concert on September 11, Pasternak came backstage to embrace Bernstein. He appeared to be unrecognized by the audience; the visitors hypothesized that the Soviet press had not run his picture in years.

After the September 11 concert it was time to be off; the Philharmonic had more touring to do. In Basel, both Noel Coward and Dr. J. Robert Oppenheimer turned up after the concert. In Athens, Bernstein found himself having dinner in the same restaurant as Adlai E. Stevenson. A firm believer in the value of such tours as the Philharmonic's to foster international understanding, Stevenson wished Bernstein Godspeed.

As a matter of fact, Bernstein has worked as hard at his ambassadorial function, at home and abroad, as at his musical one. Every concert has been preceded and followed by receptions, state dinners, and parties, at which Bernstein's presence has been *de rigeur*. At U.S. embassies abroad and at homes of sponsors here, Bernstein has tirelessly radiated good will on behalf of the Philharmonic and the U.S.A.

On rare occasions, his fund of good will has run out. In Denver, where the Philharmonic had a night off, Bernstein went to hear an outdoor band concert in a public park. A girl who had been observing him intently asked: "Aren't you Leonard Bernstein?"

Bernstein's first thought was: "I'm tired—I can't take this." He assured the young lady she was mistaken.

"Then I've lost a bet," she said. "I bet my mother twenty-five cents you were."

At this, Bernstein's conscience began nagging him. Eventually, he went looking for the girl to help her to cash her bet. She had disappeared. Bernstein brooded over the incident for days.

And it was not typical of the touring Bernstein. Usually, he is a cheerful giver of autographs ("This is part of my fun," he says) and to every question, however inane, he offers a carefully considered answer.

The only query to confound Bernstein was asked by a young lady in Atlanta: "Mr. Bernstein, what do you think of bank notes?"

Bernstein could only goggle and ask her to repeat the query.

Irrelevant questions are not the only hazard of

touring. Planes are late, instruments get mis-directed, and concerts sometimes have to be re-scheduled in such unlikely places as sports arenas and airplane hangars.

In places where concerts are infrequently given, it can almost be taken for granted that the piano will be out of tune, out of order, or both. As frequent piano soloist with the Philharmonic, this weighs heavily on Bernstein. He has won the ad-miration of orchestra men for his ability to make do with whatever turns up.

In one town, local enthusiasts wishing to have everything in order for Maestro Bernstein had applied furniture polish generously not only to the piano's case but to the keys as well. The piano shone like a new Cadillac, but fingers would not stay on the keys.

Someone in the Philharmonic party had the spe-cialized knowledge that bourbon was good for cutting grease. Generous application of this useful beverage got the keyboard in shape by concert time.

Bernstein's high spirits and sheer *joie de vivre* are evident at such moments as when he spotted a trampoline in the middle of a torch-lit patio where an after-concert party was taking place. Bernstein immediately took off his shoes and, in black tie and dinner jacket, bounced cross-legged, yogi fashion, side by side with his host's daughter.

Although the tours have meant a great deal of hard work, Bernstein has managed to have fun as well. He has gone skiing in the Chilean Andes, salmon-fishing in Puget Sound, and water-skiing on every continent.

"Lenny is unbelievable," says an associate. "He has to try everything."

At one airport, a photographer tried to pose Bernstein astride a motorcycle. Bernstein refused.

"That would be a phony," he objected. "I don't ride a motorcycle."

The photographer assured him it was so easy he could if he tried. He showed him how the controls worked. Bernstein began to be interested. In a few moments, to the consternation of horrified Philharmonic officials, he was off at top speed. Then he coaxed a Philharmonic player onto the jump seat and made another turn about the airfield.

"Now you can take the picture," Bernstein said. "I'm a motorcycle rider."

It was inevitable that on the Philharmonic's flights, Bernstein should be powerfully attracted to the pilot's compartment. In South America, some musicians were unnerved by the discovery that, crossing the highest reaches of the Andes, Bernstein had been flying the plane for twenty minutes at a time.

An even more shattering experience awaited the

237

Philharmonic in Hawaii. En route to Honolulu, their pilot announced over the loudspeaker: "Mr. Bernstein is now at the controls."

The announcement was carefully timed to coincide with their passage over a volcano. The hot blast of air created an updraft in which the musicians were shaken like dice in a box.

Although the announcement was made as a gag, the Philharmonic had no way of knowing this at the time. Under the circumstances, it was somewhat remarkable that the orchestra recovered its nerve in time to play that evening's concert.

Chapter 22

THAT NOTHING SUCCEEDS like success was shown in Bernstein's early seasons with the Philharmonic. Its board of directors could beam as they contemplated subscription sales and attendance figures. And they could take pride not only in box office results, but also in having aided the cause of international understanding, whenever the Philharmonic returned, covered with glory, from its tours.

Perhaps no one was more pleased than the musicians themselves. "The season is getting longer, we're being accepted by audiences all over the world, and we're making money," is the way one of them put it. "What more could musicians want?"

But, inevitably, there is a dissenting opinion which sees the dark side.

"What about Bernstein's responsibility to his Philharmonic subscribers?" it asks. "Sure, the musicians are happy, and will be as long as Lenny is a good provider. Between concerts, TV, and recording, the Philharmonic is one of the major jobs in the country, second only to one of those $30,000 jobs in Hollywood. But Lenny is pushing them too hard. They've been playing steadily since June. They get back from West Berlin Sunday, take Monday off, and start the winter season Tuesday. They're worn out. They'll play well for Lenny and take it out on the guest conductors."

Here it may be observed that Bernstein does not ask of the orchestra anything he is not willing to do himself—and more. The grapes need sweetening.

Still, it is a point of view found with some frequency. Many people hate Bernstein—not for personal reasons, but merely for being Leonard Bernstein, the All-American Boy of the music world. New York is full of musicians who feel themselves to have been climbing the rope ladder of life hand over hand, slipping back as often as going forward, while Bernstein has nonchalantly ridden the escalator to success, bowing right and left to acknowledge the huzzas of the multitude.

"It's easy to dislike Lenny, for obvious reasons," his wife once shrewdly observed. "He's been too lucky, too gifted, too successful."

The I-Hate-Bernstein school would go even further. His whole career, they maintain, has been a fluke, based not on solid merit but on a sort of universal stupefaction that one man would have the temerity to attempt so many things at once.

As a consequence, Bernstein has made three times as many enemies as he might have made had he been content to be merely a conductor, composer, or pianist.

This attitude of the musical community has dogged Bernstein all through his career. As early as the mid-forties, it was amusing to see what happened when one tossed his name into a conversation. Pianists would describe him as so gifted a conductor that he ought to conduct. Conductors would say his orchestral imagination was so vivid that he should stick to composing. Serious composers would say his true affinity was for jazz, while jazz men would regret his spending on jazz time that might be devoted to serious composition.

The musical world has long tried to pigeonhole Bernstein, to fit him into the compartment in which he belongs. And Bernstein time after time has frustrated these efforts by coming up with the musical equivalent of a brilliant end run or touchdown pass—a dazzling success in an unexpected area.

The musical world shakes its head. It does not know what to make of such things. There is no precedent for it.

Pianists, especially, are reluctant to grant Bernstein full membership in their fraternity, because he has never played a recital. How, they ask, can the full range and diversity of a player's style be judged, except from a solo recital? And, they add, he has expanded little over the years, from a pianistic point of view. The concertos which he conducts from the keyboard are mostly works learned during his student days.

"I don't like Lenny," says another dissenter, "but I've got to hand it to him. He has a big reputation as a composer, even though his serious works are almost never played by anybody but himself. He never had a very good press when he guest-conducted the Philharmonic and the Symphony of the Air. So he gets the Philharmonic. How does he do it?"

But the Bernstein equation is always in balance. For every detractor, there is an appreciator.

The chief reason why Bernstein has never played a recital, says the latter, is lack of time. Pianism at the highest level is a full-time, all-engrossing way of life. One does not prepare a recital with one hand while conducting with the other. But this does not at all prove Bernstein incapable of preparing a recital, if it were worth his while to do so and nothing more pressing were at hand.

Appreciators will even concede Bernstein's limitations as a conductor. Superlatively gifted at analyzing and interpreting contemporary works, he is not yet equally sure-handed in Beethoven, Haydn, Mozart, Brahms, the staples of the orchestral repertoire. What of it? they ask. In his early forties, Bernstein is young, as conductors go. He has plenty of time to ripen, to broaden, to mature with years and wisdom.

And when all is said and done, they add, he has brought new excitement to concertgoing and introduced the Philharmonic to a wider audience than it has ever had before.

As a matter of fact, Bernstein's first encounter with a Philharmonic audience, like his first encounter with his Aunt Clara's piano, was a case of love at first sight, and it has continued that way ever since.

At the Pension Fund Benefit concert of February 13, 1961, Philharmonic subscribers witnessed the unusual spectacle of Bernstein sitting in a Carnegie Hall box while others led the orchestra.

The all-Bernstein program was a tribute which the Philharmonic used to reserve for Beethoven, Brahms and sometimes Wagner. And oldest subscribers could recall no precedent for the red heart-shaped program cover which proclaimed the concert "A Valentine for Leonard Bernstein."

It was a gay, festive evening which began with Aaron Copland's spirited conducting of the Overture to *Candide*. Then the baton passed to Vladimir

243

Golschmann, who led the "Jeremiah" Symphony, with Jennie Tourel the soloist as she had been at the original New York performance. Lukas Foss next led the orchestra in a new suite of nine Symphonic Dances fashioned by Bernstein from the *West Side Story* score. The program was rounded out with scenes, staged and costumed, from *On the Town, Wonderful Town, Candide, Fancy Free,* and *West Side Story,* with Betty Comden and Adolph Green as masters of ceremonies.

Like the annual "birthday concert" of the Philadelphia Academy of Music at which Bernstein had been a guest of honor the month before, the "valentine" was a concert in holiday mood. And so impressive was its display of Bernstein's range and versatility that Ronald Eyer commented in the New York *Herald Tribune*:

> It is a good rule never to discount Lenny Bernstein in advance. If you should hear that he has invented a new skin-diving technique or has gone in for Andean archaeology, don't laugh. It is entirely possible that he has. His talents are that proliferous.

One might add that if it would be a mistake to overestimate Bernstein's talent, it would be an equal mistake to assume he has none. Reputations based on non-musical or extra-musical factors do not last long. A number of recent cases could be cited to show that the skyrocket can fall as rapidly as it ascended.

"Lenny's great gift is for analysis," a long-time associate says. "He has one of those minds that breaks a problem down into its lowest common denominators. He can put his finger instantly on what is basic and what isn't. I remember years ago hearing him rehearse a devilishly hard piece, the Chavez *Sinfonia India,* with the old New York City Symphony Orchestra. The players were having a hard time, and Lenny saw immediately what the trouble was. They were thrown off by the tricky rhythms. Lenny made them stop playing and start counting. Once they got the rhythm, everything else fell into place.

"Lenny is a born teacher. He can communicate things to people because he visualizes them himself. That's why he's good on television. That's why he's also good, say, at teaching you to water-ski. He'll tell you what you should be doing, feeling, and thinking at any given moment so graphically that he'll have you up on skis twice as fast as anybody else. He can make things clear to others because he's clarified them in his own mind."

What about Bernstein the composer? Have his attainments lived up to the promise of his early works?

On this point, it is possible to quote a well qualified observer, Bernstein himself.

"A performer," he once pointed out, "is a highly

public figure whose whole compulsion is to get out there in front of people and let it out. Now, the creative person is a whole other guy. He has a complex inner life. His big relationship is with himself or his Muse, or his God, or his unconscious. Most people of the arts belong to one group or the other. My misfortune is to live in a schizophrenic world of both."

That is well put, and recalls what Tchaikovsky wrote to his patron, Mme. von Meck, of the piano virtuoso Nicholas Rubinstein.

"He is a perfect contrast to you and me," Tchaikovsky observed. "In proportion as we love seclusion, he loves to go about the world and roar. He simply cannot live without excitement and rushing about; it is life to him. He dislikes reading, to walk bores him and he even has no pleasure in making music for himself—others must be there to listen. What can rest and tranquillity give such a man? Nothing but torture."

Tchaikovsky, the creative artist, was happiest composing; Rubinstein, the performer, was happiest performing; Bernstein, a little of both, cannot be wholly happy doing either.

And Bernstein, the composer of musicals, is still unhappy over his failure to write a genuine hit tune. "It would be nice," he has observed, "to hear someone accidentally whistle something of mine, somewhere, just once."

246

The composer who writes serious works as Vladimir Dukelsky, and popular tunes as Vernon Duke, recalls a Hollywood party given by Ira Gershwin to celebrate the première of *On the Waterfront.* A number of song writers were present, and each played his own works. Then Bernstein was prevailed upon to sit down at the piano.

"He played a few chords," Duke recalls, "and suddenly reflected that he had never written a big hit tune. He said, 'I've nothing to play—it's a terrible realization.' And he got up and walked out of the room."

Bernstein broods over other things, too. He is a busy man, a famous man, a successful man, but hardly a serene one.

"I can't understand it," said a friend of long standing. "He's busting out with talent, he makes better than $100,000 a year, and he's insecure."

Another friend was shocked by the picture on the cover of *The Joy of Music.*

"It isn't just that he's older and his hair is turning gray," she said. "He looks haggard. He looks like a twentieth-century Prometheus, with some sort of vulture tearing at his liver."

(Bernstein himself was unhappy with the picture. "I don't look *that* bad," he protested. "At least, not all the time." Publishers, however, have ways of finding out things, and it was discovered

247

this was the picture which girls in the office were hiding under their desk blotters.)

But there are always things waiting to be done. And Bernstein, like Nicholas Rubinstein, has the performer's compulsion to "get out there and let it out."

On a recent August morning, Bernstein sat in his Fifty-seventh Street apartment, staring moodily at a cup of coffee. He had gone to his rambling, old-fashioned summer home at Martha's Vineyard, planning a two-month holiday. He would sit in the sun, swim, sail his boat, play with his children, and unwind from the tensions of a hard winter season. Then, if he felt like it, he might begin writing; several ideas at the back of his mind were clamoring for attention.

The holiday began pleasantly. Bernstein and his children had a number of "inventures," which included getting lost in a swamp and being nearly eaten alive by mosquitoes.

Then the outside world began closing in. There were details to be arranged for the forthcoming Philharmonic tour. One feature was to be a telecast from West Berlin, which meant further conferences with television technicians. Rehearsals and recording sessions had to be planned . . . And Bernstein had sprained his back, that most vulnerable part of a conductor's anatomy, at water-skiing.

Now Bernstein was back in steaming Manhattan,

looking more jaded than words could say. His appetite was poor, and insomnia, that dreaded enemy of all who live on nervous energy, was taking its toll. He had slept badly for a month. That very morning, as the sun rose over midtown Manhattan, he had been at the piano, practicing, unable to sleep.

And in three days, the Philharmonic would begin a long, strenuous tour which would take it into the opening of the 1960-61 season without a break. Meanwhile, there were trunks to be packed, scores to be accounted for, and a thousand other details of preparation.

A caller came away from Bernstein's apartment depressed. The upcoming Philharmonic schedule was enough to daunt a college fullback. How could Bernstein, harassed and weary, fail to crack under the strain?

During the following weeks, reports began to come in of the Philharmonic's triumphs in Western cities.

"You need not have concerned yourself," a Philharmonic spokesman smiled. "Lenny's appetite has come back, he's sleeping like a baby, and his back doesn't hurt any more. Once the tour got under way, he was fine."

Chapter 23

ON A RECENT WEDNESDAY, Bernstein stopped the Philharmonic rehearsal punctually at half past twelve. The musicians began filing out for the lunch break.

At the stage door, a player with a violin under his arm indicated "after you" in pantomime.

"Lenny, you have such a remarkable knowledge of bowing," he said. "Do you play violin yourself?"

"You flatter me," Bernstein said. "I just go by intuition."

At the head of the stairway leading to the conductor's dressing room, two men were waiting.

"Lenny, this is my brother," one of them said. "I spoke to you about him, remember?"

"Of course," Bernstein said, shaking hands. "There's nothing doing at the moment, but I haven't forgotten you."

In the dressing room, his assistant, Jack Gottlieb, stood by as Bernstein pulled over his head his mustard-colored rehearsal shirt and put on a white shirt and tie.

"We still can't find the Prokofiev score," Gottlieb reported.

"Impossible."

"We've looked everywhere."

Bernstein frowned. "I tell you what. I must have the piano reduction somewhere. See if you can dig that out."

Gottlieb made a note.

"I have to see the doctor," Bernstein said. "This bronchitis is killing me. Jack, why don't you take orders for lunch. We'll be back in half an hour. How about one of those fat Jewish sandwiches?"

"Hot pastrami."

Gottlieb again made a note.

On the way out, a gray-haired man said something to Bernstein in a low voice.

"I haven't forgotten," Bernstein said. "It's in a pile of scores I haven't had a chance to look at. I'll let you know as soon as I can."

"Problems," Bernstein said. "Everybody has problems." He sighed. "Well, I've been in that situation myself."

Bernstein's car, a gray Lincoln convertible driven by a gray-uniformed chauffeur, was waiting at the Carnegie Hall stage door.

"Dr. Barach's, Eightieth and Park Avenue," Bernstein said. He relaxed against the red leather upholstery.

"Pardon me if my head is full of Schumann," Bernstein said. "I am proving that by meticulously balancing the dynamics, reinforcing the strings here, holding back the trumpets there, and so on, it is possible to make a Schumann symphony sound without re-orchestrating a single bar or changing a single note of the music."

"Not easy to do, with Schumann's instrumentation."

"That," said Bernstein, "is an ancient canard, which I'm refuting. Schumann the fuzzy orchestrator, Schumann the pianistically oriented composer. Actually, Schumann had a wonderful orchestral imagination. I demonstrated this at the preview the other night. With the orchestra playing excerpts, I showed what wonderful effects are in the music if you take the trouble to bring them out."

"Good for you."

"Good for Schumann. We've recorded all the symphonies for Columbia. The sound is gorgeous."

The convertible drew up at a Park Avenue marquee.

"I got this bronchitis in St. Louis, on the tour," said Bernstein. "They told me to relax, take it easy, get some rest. How am I supposed to relax?

Now I've gone to this new man and he's helped me more than anybody."

After treatment, Bernstein felt better, if not in all respects the picture of health.

"A lot of people think you're pushing yourself too hard."

"I'm going to cut down." The animation drained out of Bernstein's face, as if merely thinking about the season made him tired. "A long tour after the spring season, then another long tour running right into the fall season—nobody can keep that up. I've told them, no more. I'll do one tour, but not both. I want to conduct six weeks at the beginning of the season and six weeks at the end, as I'm doing this year. And, of course, the TV shows. Otherwise, that gives me four luxurious months in the middle of the winter, to compose, to read, to go to the theater, to just sit and think. I feel I've earned it."

"What happens to the Philharmonic during those four months?"

"That," said Bernstein, "is exactly the rub. We've set high standards for the orchestra. Discipline is good, morale is high. Only this morning the leader of one of the sections told me, 'Lenny, I don't like the way my boys are playing this passage. Maybe you better speak to them about it.' The men take pride in themselves and their playing. We don't want to lose that. The main thing is the Philharmonic."

"Will the board go along?"

"They have so far. They've given me everything I've asked."

"There was speculation over how long they could keep you, in the face of the combined lure of Broadway, television, and the movies."

"The Philharmonic can have me as long as it wants me."

(The Philharmonic is sure of him for seven years. Bernstein's contract is the longest given a conductor in this century, and it may be the longest in Philharmonic history.)

In Bernstein's dressing room, the Prokofiev score was on the table surrounded by pastrami sandwiches.

"Ideas?" Bernstein said, munching happily. "More than I have time for. I owe the Koussevitzky Foundation a commission. Officially, I can write anything I please, but unofficially I know Munch would love to have a Bernstein piano concerto with me as soloist. I owe the Library of Congress a commission for a semi-dramatic work. And I owe the Philharmonic a commission for Lincoln Center. I want to write an opera, if I can only find the right collaborator. The scene would be the eighteenth-century Polish ghetto. And I'd like to do another Broadway show—only it must be a consuming idea, not just any Broad-. way show." Bernstein stirred his coffee thoughtfully. "The main thing is to make a start. I've hardly written a note since *West Side Story*."

"How about the piano? Have you ever thought of playing a recital?"

"Often and often. But let's be realistic, that's not something you do in your spare time. Did you hear Richter the other night? Unbelievable. You hear something like that and you ask yourself, 'Who the hell do you think *you* are?' Still, the piano was my first love and always will be. The other night I was playing violin and piano sonatas with Isaac Stern. We said, 'This is fun, and we're pretty good at it. Why don't we play a sonata recital?' Maybe we will."

"How about teaching? Will you do more of it, now that you have time free?"

"I'd love to go back to Brandeis. I enjoyed it and I think the students found it stimulating."

"We did," said Gottlieb.

"Taking the long view, how do you picture your future and the Philharmonic's?"

"As far as the Philharmonic is concerned," Bernstein said reflectively, "the immediate prospect is good. All our orchestras, and not just the Philharmonic, are thriving. Where a quarter of a century ago we had half a dozen major orchestras and two dozen minor ones, now they're up in the thousands. There's public interest and support. All this is to the good—for now.

"Over the longer range, I'm somewhat pessimistic. I see two main strains in the music being written today. The works of the Boulez-Stockhausen-Cage school are essentially chamber music. Another strain is in one way or another in the *ambience* of the theater."

"Including the works of Leonard Bernstein."

"Among others. But the point is that neither of these leads into the concert hall. Now, we can go on for maybe a generation playing Bartók, Schoenberg, Hindemith, and so on and calling it 'modern music,' even though some of it is half a century old. Then what? Will audiences go on indefinitely listening to the Favorite Fifty Pieces, starting with Bach and ending with Bartók? In music, everything comes back to the composer. How long can music thrive without new composers and new ideas?"

"Music has been in the doldrums before, and survived."

"And probably will again."

"How about your own career? Ten years from now you'll be just turned fifty, an age at which a conductor is thought of as a promising young man."

"That used to be true," Bernstein said. "Not any more. A lot of younger men are coming along. Sometimes I feel positively venerable."

"Even so, conducting is a long-lived profession.

If precedent means anything, you have twenty to forty good conducting years ahead of you. Where will they take you? For instance, what will the Leonard Bernstein of 1970 be like?"

Bernstein smiled and shrugged his shoulders.

"God knows," he said.

Outside, the hall was filling up with musicians on their way to the stage. A buzzer sounded.

"I have to go," Bernstein said. "They're calling me."

He went out with the jaunty step and erect posture which make him seem taller than he is. An anxious-looking man was waiting.

"Lenny," he said, "could I speak to you a minute?"

Recordings by and of
Leonard Bernstein

COLUMBIA

BARTÓK: *Concerto for Violin*—Isaac Stern, Philharmonic, Leonard Bernstein conducting
ML 5471
MS 6140

BARTÓK: *Concerto for Orchestra*—New York violinist; New York Philharmonic, Leonard Bernstein conducting
ML 5283
MS 6002

BEETHOVEN: *Concerto for Piano No. 2 in B-flat;* BACH: *Concerto No. 1 in D Minor for Clavier* — Glenn Gould, pianist; Columbia Symphony Orchestra, Leonard Bernstein conducting
ML 5211

BEETHOVEN: *Concerto for Piano No. 3 in C Minor*—Glenn Gould, pianist; Columbia Symphony Orchestra, Leonard Bernstein conducting
ML 5418
MS 6096

259

BEETHOVEN: *Symphony No. 5 in C Minor* CL 918
—Original sketches for first movement,
New York Philharmonic, Leonard
Bernstein conducting; entire symphony,
New York Philharmonic, Bruno Walter
conducting

BEETHOVEN: *Concerto for Violin in D*— MS 6093
Isaac Stern, violinist; New York Phil- ML 5415
harmonic, Leonard Bernstein conducting

BEETHOVEN: *Symphony No. 7 in A*—New ML 5438
York Philharmonic, Leonard Bernstein MS 6112
conducting

BERLIOZ: *Excerpts from Romeo and Juliet;* ML 5570
Roman Carnival Overture—New York MS 6170
Philharmonic, Leonard Bernstein con-
ducting

BERNSTEIN: *The Age of Anxiety (Symphony* ML 4325
No. 2)—Lukas Foss, pianist; New York
Philharmonic, Leonard Bernstein con-
ducting

BERNSTEIN: *Fancy Free;* COPLAND: *El Salon* CL 920
Mexico; MILHAUD: *La Creation du*
Monde — Columbia Symphony Orches-
tra, Leonard Bernstein conducting

BERNSTEIN: *On the Town*—First complete OL 5540
recording, with Nancy Walker, Betty OS 2028
Comden, Adolph Green, John Reardon
and Chris Alexander, Leonard Bernstein conducting

BERNSTEIN: *Serenade for Violin, Strings and Percussion*—Isaac Stern, violinist; Symphony of the Air, Leonard Bernstein conducting — ML 5144

BERNSTEIN: *Candide*—Original cast recording, with Max Adrian, Robert Rounseville, and Barbara Coo, Samuel Krachmalnick conducting — OL 5180

BERNSTEIN: *Peter Pan*—Original cast recording — OL 4312

BERNSTEIN: *West Side Story*—Original cast recording, with Carol Lawrence, Larry Kert, and Chita Rivera, Max Goberman conducting — OL 5320 / OS 2001

BERNSTEIN: *Wonderful Town*—Original cast recording, with Rosalind Russell, Sydney Chaplin, Jacquelyn McKeever, Lehman Engel conducting — OL 5360 / OS 2008

BLOCH: *Sacred Service*—Robert Merrill, cantor; New York Philharmonic, Leonard Bernstein conducting — ML 5621 / MS 6221

BRAHMS: *Symphony No. 1 in C Minor*—New York Philharmonic, Leonard Bernstein conducting — ML 5602 / MS 6202

BRUBECK: *Bernstein Plays Brubeck Plays Bernstein*—Howard Brubeck's *Dialogues for Jazz Combo and Orchestra* with Leonard Bernstein at the piano; Leonard Bernstein songs played by Dave Brubeck Quartet — CL 1466 / CS 8257

COPLAND: *Four Dance Episodes from Rodeo; Billy the Kid Ballet Suite*—New York Philharmonic, Leonard Bernstein conducting　　ML 5575

COPLAND: *The Second Hurricane*—Soloists and chorus of the New York High School of Music and Art; New York Philharmonic, Leonard Bernstein conducting　　ML 5581　MS 6181

DIAMOND: *Symphony No. 4*—New York Philharmonic, Leonard Bernstein conducting　　ML 5412　MS 6089

FRANCK: *Symphony in D Minor*—New York Philharmonic, Leonard Bernstein conducting　　ML 5391　MS 6072

GERSHWIN: *Rhapsody in Blue; An American in Paris*—New York Philharmonic, Leonard Bernstein, conductor-pianist　　ML 5413　MS 6091

HANDEL: *Ode to St. Cecilia's Day*—Adele Addison, soprano; John McCollum, tenor; John Wummer, flutist; Laszlo Varga, cellist; Bruce Prince-Joseph, organist; Rutgers University Choir; New York Philharmonic, Leonard Bernstein conducting　　ML 5606　MS 6206

HANDEL: *The Messiah (Christmas Music)*—Adele Addison, soprano; Russell Oberlin, counter-tenor; David Lloyd, tenor; William Warfield, baritone; Westminster Choir; New York Philharmonic, Leonard Bernstein conducting　　ML 5300　MS 6020

HANDEL: *The Messiah (Easter Music)*—Same artists as above   ML 5346
MS 6041

HAYDN: *Symphony No. 104 in D ("London")* —New York Philharmonic, Leonard Bernstein conducting   ML 5349
MS 6050

HILL: *Prelude for Orchestra;* LOPATNIKOFF: *Concertino for Orchestra;* DALLAPIC-COLA: *Tartiniana for Violin and Orchestra*—Ruth Posselt, violinist; Columbia Symphony Orchestra, Leonard Bernstein conducting   ML 4996

IVES: *Symphony No. 2*—New York Philharmonic, Leonard Bernstein conducting   KL 5489
KS 6155

MAHLER: *Kindertotenlieder; Four Songs*— Jennie Tourel, mezzo-soprano; New York Philharmonic, Leonard Bernstein conducting   ML 5590
MS 6197

MAHLER: *Symphony No. 4 in G*—Reri Grist, soprano; New York Philharmonic, Leonard Bernstein conducting   ML 5485
MS 6152

MENDELSSOHN: *Symphony No. 4 in A ("Italian")*—New York Philharmonic, Leonard Bernstein conducting   ML 5349
MS 6050

MOZART: *Piano Concerto No. 17 in G; Concerto No. 15 in B-Flat*—Columbia Symphony Orchestra, Leonard Bernstein, conductor-pianist   ML 5145

Moussorgsky: *Pictures at an Exhibition;*   ML 5401
Rimsky-Korsakov: *Capriccio Espagnol*   MS 6080
—New York Philharmonic, Leonard
Bernstein conducting

Prokofiev: *Violin Concerto No. 2 in G*   ML 5243
Minor—Isaac Stern, violinist; New York
Philharmonic, Leonard Bernstein con-
ducting

Prokofiev: *Peter and the Wolf;* Tchai-   ML 5593
kovsky: *Nutcracker Suite*—New York   MS 6193
Philharmonic, Leonard Bernstein, conductor and narrator

Rachmaninoff: *Piano Concerto No. 2 in*   ML 5481
C Minor—Philippe Entremont, pianist;   MS 6148
New York Philharmonic, Leonard
Bernstein conducting

Ravel: *Bolero; La Valse; Rhapsodie*   ML 5293
Espagnol — New York Philharmonic,
Leonard Bernstein conducting

Ravel: *Piano Concerto in G;* Shostako-   ML 5337
vitch: *Piano Concerto No. 2*—New   MS 6043
York Philharmonic, Leonard Bernstein,
conductor and pianist

Rimsky-Korsakov: *Scheherazade*—New York   ML 5387
Philharmonic, Leonard Bernstein con-   MS 6069
ducting

Shapero: *Symphony for Classical Orches-*   ML 4889
tra—Columbia Symphony Orchestra,
Leonard Bernstein conducting

264

SHOSTAKOVITCH: *Symphony No. 5*—New York Philharmonic, Leonard Bernstein conducting | ML 5445
MS 6115

STRAVINSKY: *Firebird Suite;* TCHAIKOVSKY: *Romeo and Juliet*—New York Philharmonic, Leonard Bernstein conducting | ML 5182
MS 6014

STRAVINSKY: *Le Sacre du Printemps*—New York Philharmonic, Leonard Bernstein conducting | ML 5277
MS 6010

TCHAIKOVSKY: *Symphony No. 4 in F Minor* —New York Philharmonic, Leonard Bernstein conducting | ML 5332
MS 6035

Humor in Music—New York Philharmonic, Leonard Bernstein conducting | ML 5625
MS 6225

Overture!—New York Philharmonic, Leonard Bernstein conducting | ML 5623
MS 6223

What Is Jazz?—From Leonard Bernstein's *Omnibus* series | CL 919

RCA VICTOR

Recordings marked with asterisk (*) are no longer in the catalogue.

BERNSTEIN: *On the Town Excerpts*—Original cast, Leonard Bernstein conducting | CAL 196

BERNSTEIN: *Jeremiah Symphony* — Nan Merriman, contralto; St. Louis Symphony Orchestra, Leonard Bernstein conducting | CAL 196

BERNSTEIN: *Facsimile*—RCA Victor Orchestra, Leonard Bernstein conducting   CAL 196

BERNSTEIN: *Seven Anniversaries* — Leonard Bernstein, pianist   *CAL 351

BLITZSTEIN: *Airborne Symphony*—Robert Shaw, narrator; RCA Victor Chorale; New York City Symphony, Leonard Bernstein conducting   *M 1117

COPLAND: *Billy the Kid*—RCA Victor Orchestra, Leonard Bernstein conducting   CAL 439

COPLAND: *Sonata for Piano*—Leonard Bernstein, pianist   *CAL 214

GERSHWIN: *An American in Paris* — RCA Victor Orchestra, Leonard Bernstein conducting   CAL 439

RAVEL: *Piano Concerto*—Recorded in England; Leonard Bernstein, conductor-pianist   *CAL 214

STRAVINSKY: *L'Histoire du Soldat; Octet for Wind Instruments* — Boston Symphony Orchestra, Leonard Bernstein conducting   *LMX 1078

DECCA (VOCALION)

BERNSTEIN: *Wonderful Town*—Original cast recording   DL 9010

BERNSTEIN: *West Side Story*—Jazz interpretation by Manny Alban and his Orchestra   VL 3678

266

BERNSTEIN: *On the Town Excerpts*—Orig-   DL 803
   inal cast recording

MGM

BERNSTEIN: *Trouble in Tahiti* — Original   MGM 3646
   television cast recording

MUSIC APPRECIATION RECORDS

These two-disk sets, each consisting of a recorded symphony and a companion disk of analysis and comment
by Bernstein, are available only from the Book-of-the-
Month Club. In all five recordings, Bernstein conducts
the Stadium Concerts Symphony Orchestra.

BEETHOVEN: *Symphony No. 3 in E-flat, Op. 55 ("Eroica")*

BRAHMS: *Symphony No. 4 in E Minor, Op. 98*

DVORAK: *Symphony No. 5 in E Minor, Op. 95, "From the
New World"*

SCHUMANN: *Symphony No. 2 in C, Op. 61*

TCHAIKOVSKY: *Symphony No. 6 in B Minor, Op. 74
("Pathétique")*

WARNER BROTHERS

BERNSTEIN: *West Side Story*—The Prince   B 1240
   Orchestra

267

INDEX

269

271

272

THIS BOOK WAS SET IN

BASKERVILLE AND PALATINO TYPES BY

SLUGS COMPOSITION COMPANY.

IT WAS BOUND AT THE PRESS OF

THE WORLD PUBLISHING COMPANY.

DESIGN IS BY LARRY KAMP

Jacket Photographs

FRONT. Photo by Eugene Cook
SPINE. Photo by courtesy of The Baldwin Piano Company
BACK. Photo by courtesy of Columbia Records